China Nurse

The Life Story of Elisabeth Redelstein

by Mary S. Ogle

PACIFIC PRESS PUBLISHING ASSOCIATION
Mountain View, California
Omaha, Nebraska   Oshawa, Ontario

Library of Congress Catalog Card No. 74-79164

Dedicated

To my sister Florence and to all those other "angels in white" who, like her and Elisabeth Redelstein, have expended their life's energies in compassionately caring for the sick and suffering.

Contents

1
War Crimes Trials

Elisabeth Redelstein glanced at the name the American Army officer handed her. Startled, she took a closer look. The name fairly leaped off the paper–Alexander von Falkenhausen. Before her mind's eye stood a tall military figure in full German army uniform. "Major," she asked in her heavy German-accented English, "is this the same General von Falkenhausen who served as an adviser to Chiang Kai-shek in China?"

"The same," the American replied.

"Then I'm sorry, but I can't do it. The last time I saw von Falkenhausen was at a farewell party he gave for me in his home in Nanking when I was leaving Madame Chiang's employment. And I certainly cannot confront him this morning as an interpreter when he is being interrogated as a war-crimes criminal!"

"Well, I can understand that," the Major replied. "We'll give you another assignment. How about this name, does it mean anything to you?"

"No," she said, looking at the slip of paper he'd handed her. "I don't know anyone by that name."

"Then be in Room 201 at ten o'clock when this man is called in for preliminary interrogation."

The Nürnberg war-crimes trials were about to get under way. The Palace of Justice, a veritable city in itself, buzzed with excitement as the American, British, Russian, and French who had recently descended on the city prepared to swing into action. It was October, 1945, as judges, attorneys, court reporters, interpreters, translators, secretaries, and stenographers gathered for the trials. A heterogeneous group, they were made up of military personnel, most of whom spoke little or no German. And there was also an odd assortment of carefully screened bilingual interpreters and translators. Elisabeth was one of these.

She, along with fifty other Americans, was temporarily billeted in the Grand Hotel. The front of the old hotel still stood, looking rather imposing in the midst of surrounding rubble. But inside a whole section had collapsed under a freak bombing. Board planks across the gaping hole provided a bridge for the Americans to cross from the front section to their billet quarters. With breakfast in the nearby Army mess hall, lunch in the courthouse cafeteria, and dinner at the Grand Hotel, Elisabeth realized she would be well fed and as well housed as conditions in the country made possible.

Elisabeth had arrived last Thursday. A middle-aged woman with gray hair combed straight back in a rather severe style, she had quickly been caught up in the pretrial procedures.

Friday had been processing day. Elisabeth and the other recruits went from one room to another, being fingerprinted, receiving ID cards, courthouse passes, et cetera. In one room a bulletin board announced: SUNDAY, EXCURSION TO STUTTGART. THIRTY PEOPLE CAN GO. SIGN HERE IF YOU WISH TO GO. Stuttgart! The home of many of her relatives. Surely she could find some of them and learn if her mother was still alive! Quickly she signed her name.

All during this morning of processing one thought kept ticking away in the back of Elisabeth's mind—"There is something I must take care of before this day is over." In the afternoon, Colonel Williams, the very man she wanted to see, walked into the office where she was. "Colonel Williams—" she approached him— "may I have a few moments of your time?"

"Surely, Miss Redelstein. Do you want to come to my office, or can we talk here?"

"I can say what I have to say right here. Colonel Williams, I am a Seventh-day Adventist. I don't know whether you know anything about Adventists—"

"Oh, yes, I do," the colonel interrupted. "My grandfather was an Adventist, and I suppose by rights I ought to be one too."

"Then you know that I shall want to be excused from work on the Sabbath."

"We don't work here on Saturday anyway unless something very important comes up. So don't worry, you won't have any trouble about your Sabbath."

On Sunday morning Jeeps lined up in front of the Grand Hotel to take on passengers for the excursion to Stuttgart. First in the queue of excursionists, Elisabeth and another lady got into the first Jeep along with a sergeant who introduced himself as Sergeant Zucker, excursion leader. With an American GI at the wheel, they bumped over pot-holed streets and out of the city along country roads. Spotting a farmer in a field, the sergeant asked the driver to stop. He got out and talked with the man. Elisabeth heard him asking about a certain bridge, whether it was possible to cross or whether the bridge had been blown up.

"Sergeant Zucker," she declared when he came back to the Jeep, "you didn't learn your German in America!"

The sergeant laughed. "What makes you think that?"

"I heard you talking to that man, and I know that was real 'German' German."

"No, Miss Redelstein. I was a teacher in a Jewish school in Stuttgart for years, and I have ridden my motorcycle all over this territory on vacations. That is why I was asked to lead this excursion. I know the area very well. My mother has been taken to a concentration camp, and I am here trying to find her."

"And I am here to try to find out if my mother is still alive," Elisabeth said. Immediately a bond of friendship linked the German Jew and the German American. "I am a Seventh-day Adventist," Elisabeth told the sergeant. "I keep the same day you do." The bond of fellowship strengthened.

"How will I find my people, the city is so changed?" Elisabeth asked as they entered the outskirts of Stuttgart.

"We'll go to the police station. Everybody is registered there." Sergeant Zucker piloted her to the police station, and sure enough there was the name and address of a cousin. Putting her on the street car, the sergeant told the conductor where she wanted to go.

"That is almost the end of the line," the conductor said.

Elisabeth squeezed herself back into the streetcar, where people were already pressed together. "Well, at least there's no danger of falling," she thought. The passengers' sidelong glances cast at her WAC (Women's Army Corps) uniform made her uncomfortable. Eventually people began getting off until it was easier to breathe. She moved to a seat where a man she thought she recognized was sitting. She was sure the man was the husband of one of her cousins. She moved over to him and asked, "Are you Attorney Strohm?"

"Yes," the man replied. "And who are you?" He, too, eyed her uniform with suspicion.

"I am Elli Redelstein."

"No! That is not possible!"

"Yes. I am Elli Redelstein, and I want to know if my mother is still alive."

"Yes," Attorney Strohm told her. "I just took my wife to the station, and she's on her way to Ochsenhausen, where your mother is living in her own home."

"Oh, thank the Lord! Thank you." Elisabeth grasped the man's hand and shook it up and down. "That's the first word I've had about my mother in all the long, weary war years."

Attorney Strohm took Elisabeth to the home of another cousin, where relatives and neighbors came flocking to see her. "Elli–" they hugged her tightly–"how do you happen to be here?" Then drawing back, "What are you doing in the uniform of the enemy? Have you turned against your Fatherland?"

Patiently, Elisabeth explained the work she was doing with the American Army. "The reason I took this job," she told them, "was so I could find you; so I could learn if Mother is alive and how she is."

Then with tears and smiles and rejoicing, they filled her in on how the family had fared during the war. "How can I get in touch with Mother?" she wanted to know.

"There is no inter-zonal mail service, but cousin Martha's husband is the medical officer in charge of a certain section which is partly in the American Sector, where he lives, and partly in the French Sector, where your mother lives. If you'll write a letter to the doctor in the American Sector, he will take it to your mother in the French Sector. Then she can give him a letter for you to be mailed in the American Sector."

It seemed like a good idea, and so with the doctor's name and address tucked safely in her purse, Elisabeth met Sergeant Zucker at five o'clock and joined the caravan of Jeeps back to Nürnberg. "Oh, I am so thankful," she bubbled, "that I've learned this good news about my mother. And so soon–on my third day in Germany. Thank you so much for helping me to locate my family. I hope you will soon be successful in tracing *your* mother."

And now it was Monday. The war-crimes trials began with preliminary interrogations in separate little rooms. Within a few days, however, everything was transferred to the courtroom. The panel of judges, two from each of the four allied countries, sat on the bench. In glass-walled booths two interpreters for each country listened to the proceedings through earphones, and translated into the language of the judges to whom they were wired. Twenty of the "top brass" were tried first. They were allowed to choose their own lawyers, and they chose the best lawyers in Nazi Germany.

After the first session Elisabeth went to the colonel in charge of interpreters and translators and said, "I don't think I'm going to be able to take this. It upsets me terribly to sit through these proceedings and listen to my countrymen being accused of the terrible deeds they have done."

"Well, we need only a few people on this job anyway," the

colonel said. "But we need a lot of translators, so you can join the translation staff." He took her to the large room where the crew of translators worked. The room was filled with many pairs of desks facing each other. The colonel introduced her to Mr. Fred Lax, a Jew from New York, who worked at the desk opposite her.

The translating work was exacting, but not the emotional strain that courtroom interpreting had been. The translators struggled over documents from various sections of the German military and the government–army, air force, navy, and the Justice Department. By the time they became familiar with the terminology of one section, they were given documents from another section to translate. One Monday morning her Jewish co-worker remarked, "Miss Redelstein, you must have a very large bank account in America."

"What makes you think that?"

"Well, you never work on Saturday when we get double pay."

Elisabeth laughed. She valued the Sabbath more than money.

As Elisabeth and her fellow translators walked the corridors of the Palace of Justice, they often commented about the magnificence of the building–its paneled walls, its art objects, and most of all, the beautiful chandeliers, so designed that the shadow of the intricate pattern was cast on the ceiling above.

One cold winter day as the group paused for their afternoon break, Mr. Lax said, "This building is a monument to the accuracy of the American bombers. They knew this was a special building and purposefully avoided hitting it. There is no other explanation for its still standing undamaged. But–" he cuddled his teapot in his hands– "I'd gladly trade this for a heated shanty."

"We do look like a lot of Eskimos, don't we?" Elisabeth chuckled, looking around the room. There they sat, wearing the wool zip-in linings from their field coats, sitting on their army blankets with the ends wrapped across their laps, their feet encased in four-buckle arctics, drinking hot drinks and warming their hands on the steaming porcelain pots—a group of Americans accustomed to central heating!

Elisabeth read the sign on the bulletin board: TEN-DAY CHRISTMAS VACATION, BEGINNING DECEMBER 20. NO AMERICANS CAN TRAVEL OUTSIDE THE AMERICAN ZONE EXCEPT THE DIRECT TRAIN TRIP TO PARIS.

"Only to Paris!" she exclaimed. "I don't want to go to Paris. I want to go to see my mother." Silently she prayed, "Dear Lord, you know my whole purpose in coming to Germany was so I could see my mother. Please, if it is Your will, somehow open the way for me to go."

Later that day she saw a friend of hers, a Jewish woman lawyer of the American delegation. "What is the matter, Elisabeth?" the lawyer asked. "You don't look your usual happy self today."

"The Christmas leave regulations specify that we can't travel outside the American Sector except to Paris, and I want to see my mother at Ochsenhausen in the French Sector."

"Well, there are many ways to get around military regulations," her friend encouraged. "Come on, I'll go with you to see the head of the French delegation."

Able to speak fluent French, Elisabeth told her story and showed the officer the two copies of her travel pass as far as Ulm. He took the papers, handed them to his secretary and said, "Insert a carbon and type on here: 'The French delegation to the War Crimes Trials hereby requests the authorities of the French occupation territory to assist Miss Elisabeth Redelstein, a member of the American delegation to the War Crimes Trials, in every way possible in the carrying out of her mission.' " The officer signed the order, stamped it with the official stamp, and handed it back to her. "There you are," he smiled. "That ought to do it."

"Merci, merci!" Elisabeth thanked him. "And thank you, Father," she prayed.

The evening of December 22 she started out. Struggling aboard the train with her suitcase and a large bag of food and

Christmas presents purchased at the PX, she found a seat in an eight-passenger compartment. The compartment already had seven young GI occupants, on their way to Paris. The young men welcomed her, shuffling their gear around to make room for her baggage. "How do you think you will get that through the French territory?" they teased. "The French are great confiscators."

"I think I'll make it all right," she said with a smile.

As the train rumbled on through the cold night, the passengers huddled closer and closer together in their fitful sleeping. The cold wind swirled the snow about the train, and piled it up on the windows. The powdery snow sifted in through the cracks.

Elisabeth had been told that she would have to go by way of Stuttgart to Ulm. At Ulm she would change trains for Ochsenhausen. "I can't understand why it's taking so long to reach Stuttgart," she told the boys over and over during the long night. "It isn't that far from Nürnberg."

At last they stopped at a little station on the outskirts of Stuttgart. It was early morning, and the cold gray of winter coated the train windows. As the minutes ticked away Elisabeth grew more and more restless to get on to Ulm. Finally she asked the conductor, "When are we going to arrive at Stuttgart?"

"Madam, this *is* Stuttgart. The main station has been bombed out. This is as far as we go," he said. "We're a through train to Paris. If you want to get off at Stuttgart, you'd better get off here."

"A through train to Paris!" Almost beside herself, she gathered up her baggage and Christmas presents, and climbed off the train. "When does the train leave for Ulm?" she asked the station manager.

"The train for Ulm left on that track five minutes ago."

"When does the next train go?"

"Tomorrow morning."

"Tomorrow morning! To think that I just sat there while the train was taking off for Ulm," Elisabeth fumed to herself. After a moment of disappointment, she decided to make the most of her time in Stuttgart. She telephoned her cousin and spent the day and the night with her. The next morning she was on her way to Ulm.

Again passengers looked curiously at her big bag of food. "How will you ever get through the French zone with all that?" they asked.

"Wait and see," was all she could say. That was what she had to do too. When Elisabeth told the trainmen in Ulm that she'd gone to Stuttgart on her way from Nürnberg, they laughed. "Why, you passed through Ulm in the night," they said.

"So much for misunderstandings in the Army!" Elisabeth shook her head in disappointment at having wasted a whole day that could have been spent with her mother.

On the last lap of her journey home, the train's narrow-gauge track twisted and looped its way around the hills from Ulm to Ochsenhausen. Elisabeth could hardly wait to see her mother. This train was colder than the others had been. The snow fell thicker and thicker, and the little engine puffed its way up hills and around curves. Midway on that run the French occupation soldiers boarded to check passengers going into French territory. Elisabeth spoke to them in French and showed them the order from the head of the French delegation in Nürnberg. After reading that order the soldiers treated her courteously.

At ten o'clock the train stopped at Ochsenhausen. Elisabeth arrived twenty-four hours late at her old hometown. There to meet her was the refugee woman who lived with her mother. The woman had met the train the night before, but when Elisabeth did not get off, she came back tonight with a little cart for Elisabeth's baggage.

The falling snow spread a sparkling white blanket over the town. It blotted out the scars of war, creating a perfect Christmas-card scene as Elisabeth and the woman trudged up the moonlit street.

Elisabeth's heart pounded painfully, she was so excited. After all those violent years, she was going to see her mother. The door opened. The light from the lamps streamed out onto the snow. And there stood her mother! Elisabeth and her mother embraced. Tears streamed down their faces. They were together again, at last.

Wiping their eyes, they went inside to catch up on all that had happened during the eight years since they had last seen each other.

As on Christmas eves of old, they sang carols, read the Christ Child's story, and prayed together, thanking God not only for that first Christmas gift, but also for this happy reunion.

Elisabeth's supplements from her big bag made a real Christmas dinner out of her mother's frugal meal. "Without these goodies," her mother said, "this would have been one of the poorest Christmases we've ever known. But how rich we are to have the knowledge of a loving and soon-coming Saviour."

Their few days together rushed past like an express train. Elisabeth tried to grasp and hold each precious moment, savoring the companionship of her mother. But far too soon, she was heading back to Nürnberg through the gusty snow of Germany's winter.

In the weeks that followed, the women workers were moved out of the Grand Hotel and billeted in a group of suburban houses which the military had taken over. Two German girls were hired to keep house for each group of women in their own billet. Elisabeth was billet leader for the ten young women who shared the house with her. She was responsible to the billeting officer and reported to him any needs or difficulties. She was also the go-between for the maids and the other girls in the billet.

One spring evening, the second year of her stay in Germany, as Elisabeth left the house on her way to the English class she taught twice a week, one of the maids stopped her. "Miss Redelstein, Miss Leavy has been sick all day. I have heard her moaning and groaning."

"I will look in on her when I get back," Elisabeth promised and went on to her class. When she returned two hours later, both maids came running to her apartment, crying, "Why did she have to kill it? Why did she have to kill it? We would have taken care of it."

"What are you talking about?" Elisabeth demanded.

"I heard a baby cry in Miss Leavy's room," one maid explained. "Just then I heard Maria coming home, and I ran to tell her—"

"We ran to her room and rapped on the door and told her we'd help her," the other maid took up the story. "But the door was locked, and she told us to go away and leave her alone. Oh, why did she have to kill it?"

As billet leader and as a trained nurse, Elisabeth thought she had better investigate. The young woman denied having given birth. "Listen, young lady, I'm a nurse. You can't fool me on something like that," Elisabeth said. "You probably need some attention, and I can help you." The woman relaxed and Elisabeth took care of her. But the woman refused to let anyone touch the bundle of newspapers in the corner of her room.

"And I thought she was just getting careless about her appearance!" Elisabeth said to herself. Later she was able to get some medicine for the woman from a Seventh-day Adventist doctor in the U.S. Army.

The doctor sighed when Elisabeth told him the circumstances. "We have many similar cases all the time," he said.

Working all day in the courthouse, teaching English two evenings a week, and supervising the women in her billet kept Elisabeth busy.

As the months and years passed, Elisabeth visited her mother on every holiday granted the American delegates.

When she arrived at her mother's home on the George Washington Birthday leave in 1948, she found her mother very sick.

Her mother was in bed; a weak smile crossed her features when she saw Elisabeth.

The next day, at the close of Sabbath, Elisabeth sat beside

the bed, holding her mother's hand, and watched as the elderly woman slipped quietly away.

"Oh, dear God," Elisabeth prayed, "thank You for giving me these last few years with my mother. Thank You for letting me be with her at death."

2

Food Bags and Bibles

Not long after the trials began, Sergeant Zucker came to Elisabeth's desk with a newspaper clipping in his hand. "Miss Redelstein," he said, "here's a notice of church services to be held on Saturday. It must be your church. I'm sure it isn't Jewish."

"Thank you very much, Sergeant Zucker. I've been wondering how I would ever locate a Seventh-day Adventist church in Nürnberg with most of the city completely bombed out," Elisabeth said. "I'll look up this address."

Saturday morning she called the motor pool and asked for a car to take her to one of the suburbs. Arriving at the address, she saw people entering a hall. She followed them across a courtyard and into a little back room. A sawdust-burning stove stood in the center of the room valiantly striving to produce a little heat. People huddled around the stove rubbing their hands. As she entered, they turned and stared at her. Elisabeth smiled, but received only faint smiles and raised eyebrows in return. Knowing looks passed between the people around the stove. "My uniform again," she said to herself.

Before she could introduce herself, the meeting was called to order, and she took a seat on the back row. But after the services, she spoke to the pastor. "I have a letter from the General Conference in Washington, D.C., for our people here," she told him. "Can you give me the name and address of the leader of our work in Germany so I can pass the letter on to him? I've already translated it into German."

At first the pastor eyed her with suspicion, but finally he gave her the name and address of the conference president in Nürnberg. Later that afternoon she visited the conference president. He gave her the name of the headquarters office in Berlin.

"I feel now that I've accomplished my two missions in coming to Germany," Elisabeth told him. "I found my mother, and now I have made contact with our church."

The next day she sent on to the leader in Berlin the letter from W. H. Branson, vice-president of the General Conference. This was the first communication the church in Germany had had from the church in America during the four years of the war.

Soon she received a reply from the leaders in Berlin, which she translated into English and sent on to Elder Branson. This was the first word the church in America had had from the church in Germany for the same long four years.

"There is a church near here," the conference president told her. "You don't need to go clear out there to the suburb to church. We're meeting in one of the rooms of the Lutheran church. The secretary of educational and religious affairs of the occupation forces assigned it to us. It's right near the Grand Hotel."

From then on Elisabeth attended the church near the Grand Hotel. When the church members realized that she was really one of them and not a traitor to her Fatherland, they opened their hearts to her.

When she realized that the German believers had been worshiping all through the war years with almost no Bibles and no *Sabbath School Lesson Quarterlies,* she determined to change the situation. The pastor had simply been reading a portion of Scripture from his Bible and then the believers discussed it as their Sabbath School lesson.

When the conference president and his wife invited Elisabeth to their house for Sabbath dinner, she took along some food items that she had purchased at the PX.

After the meal she handed the young son a chocolate candy bar. The boy took the candy bar as though it were something precious. Carefully cutting it into three exact pieces, he handed one to his mother and one to his father before tasting it himself. "We haven't tasted anything like this for so long!" the mother exclaimed. "I'd almost forgotten what chocolate tasted like."

Tears stung Elisabeth's eyes as she saw the father take a teaspoon and carefully scrape from the candy wrapper the tiny fragments of chocolate that clung to it.

Elisabeth began writing to friends in America, telling them how greatly food and clothing were needed. Direct mail service was still impossible between Germany and the outside world. But through her APO address Elisabeth became the bridge over which flowed a heavy traffic of letters and parcels from concerned relatives and church members in America to people in Germany.

As soon as packages began arriving, she took them to the conference president's office. Then he distributed them to church members.

One Sabbath another family invited her home for dinner. They stopped before a house that looked completely ruined. The husband led them through what looked like a hole in the wall, but there was a door leading into a room that served as kitchen and living room. Another room was also fairly intact. The family used it for the bedroom.

"We don't have much," the mother said, "but we're so thankful to be able to live in our own house. So many people have lost everything and have had to move in with strangers or non-Christian relatives."

Noting another door, Elisabeth asked, "Where does that door lead?" The husband opened it, and there she saw a sheer drop-off.

"We keep this door locked," he said. The rest of the house had simply been torn away by a bomb explosion.

"We're so thankful for the food you've brought us. We've always had bread and water, and that is what the Lord promised. But now it is so nice to have something to spread on our bread!" The wife smiled as she spread Crisco on her bread.

In the next few weeks other American Army uniforms began to appear in church on Sabbath. Seventh-day Adventist American GI's had somehow learned that an American Adventist woman who could translate from German into English was attending church. Between six and a dozen GI's showed up for church every Sabbath.

They sat on the back row and Elisabeth stood in front of them and gave a running translation of the sermon preached in German. Some of the boys had English *Sabbath School Lesson Quarterlies,* and so they had their own Sabbath School class. The German believers looked on enviously at those lesson quarterlies.

"Why don't you boys come to my billet for Sabbath lunch and spend the afternoon with me?" Elisabeth invited one Sabbath.

"That would be great!" one said, his Texas accent drawling. "How about it, fellows?" He turned to the others.

"Great!" they all agreed.

"We always get some snacks from the PX on Friday to tide us over Sabbath," another volunteered. "And we can bring them along."

And so began a warm fellowship between the middle-aged woman and the homesick young men. Every Sabbath they came bringing their sacks of crackers, cheese, fruit, and candy bars.

After lunch, they would relax in her three-room apartment on the top floor of her billet. Eagerly they read the church papers from home, discussed what they read, or listened to Elisabeth tell about her years in China.

Sabbath afternoons were also the time for letter writing. Elisabeth and the soldiers wrote home to friends, telling them of the needs of the people and urging them to send food and clothing. Parcels weighing up to seventy-two pounds could be sent to each APO address.

"Look, boys, our members are asking more for Bibles than

for anything else," Elisabeth said one Sabbath. "Now, the Americans would have to have a request from here in order to be able to mail Bibles to Germany. I'll tell you what I'll do. I'll write a notice setting forth the need for German Bibles. I will have it duplicated in my office, and each one of you sign a notice and give your serial number and APO address. Give your signed notices to me, and I'll send them to friends in America. I'm sure we can get some German Bibles for our people."

Within weeks the Bibles began arriving. Elisabeth delivered them to the conference president's office. German Bibles were not the only thing that began arriving. Soon, so many seventy-two-pound packages of food and clothing were coming addressed to Elisabeth that she came under suspicion.

One day when she went to the courthouse postoffice to collect a large shipment, the postal clerk said, "Miss Redelstein, I think I should warn you that the CIC is investigating you."

"Why? What have I done?"

"Well, you know the regulation is that each person connected with the Army is to receive from America only what he needs for his personal use. You have to admit you're getting more parcels than you can possibly use for yourself. The CIC has been asking me about it. I told them that if they were looking for black-market goods they were barking up the wrong tree. I just thought I should let you know."

Days and weeks went by. The CIC never questioned Elisabeth. And the packages continued to come.

It was one thing to ship seventy-two-pound packages from America. But distributing those goods in Germany was quite another matter. There was no parcel post service in Germany at that time, only letter mail. And letters were limited to 500 grams, approximately sixteen ounces.

To help her reduce the seventy-two-pound packages into one-pound packages, Elisabeth hired a German girl as her secretary. She also asked Barbara and Maria, the maids at her billet, if they would like to help, and she paid them in goods for their services.

Every Sunday afternoon this crew gathered in Elisabeth's living room to sort and pack about forty one-pound packages. Without a scales, it took some guessing to produce a package that weighed no more than sixteen ounces. Several parcels came back marked "overweight," until someone showed Elisabeth how to make a coat-hanger scales. Two bars of Ivory soap weighed one pound. So by tying two bars of soap on one side of the hanger, they could balance the other side with a package of food and thus know when it was within limits.

Letters began coming from people saying the package addressed to them had arrived but was empty. Mail clerks in Germany were just as hungry as any of the other citizens of the war-ravaged country. It didn't take much ingenuity to figure out that by poking a finger in the package the contents of beans, rice, flour, or sugar could be drained off.

How to prevent this posed a real problem. Then Elisabeth got the idea of buying all the khaki square handkerchiefs in the PX. The maids sewed these together into square bags, leaving only one corner open. Through that opening they filled the bag with one pound of dry ingredients and then tied the hole.

"This is a great idea!" the maids said.

Then Elisabeth asked the cleaning woman in the courthouse to gather and save all the empty Kleenex boxes from the offices. By cutting a box in two, crosswise, the two sides could be pushed one into the other. A one-pound package in a handkerchief bag just fit into the reinforced Kleenex box, and the postal clerks found it more difficult to poke a finger through the double cardboard and the cloth bag inside.

From all parts of the United States the packages came, not only from Adventist welfare societies and from other Adventists who had families in Germany, but also from non-Adventists who had families in Germany and who had learned about Elisabeth's distribution service. Clothing was almost more of a problem than food. A pair of shoes weighed more than a pound, and so each shoe had to be sent separately. A suit weighed too much. Elisabeth wrapped the trousers or skirt in one package and the jacket in another. If the jacket weighed too much, she ripped out the sleeves and sent them separately.

Before long Elisabeth had twenty-five names on her list to whom she was sending packages regularly. Her German secretary kept a record of just what was sent to each name. "This is tiring work," Elisabeth said one evening after several hours making mail packages. "But it's *so* satisfying to know I'm helping."

After about a year, the postal clerk came to Elisabeth's office one morning and with tongue in cheek said, "Miss Redelstein, surely you must be selling on the black market now."

"Why, what makes you say that? You know I never deal on the black market!"

"Then how do you explain six mail bags full of boxes all the same size that arrived this morning?"

"I don't know. Let me see what is in them!"

Hurrying to the mail room, she examined the boxes and cried out, "Bibles! German Bibles! *New* German Bibles!" An accompanying letter explained that the General Conference had ordered the Bibles from the American Bible Society to be shipped direct. Elisabeth stood looking at those six heavy mail bags with two large cartons of Bibles in each.

"How do you think you are going to get them out of here?" the postal clerk asked.

"I don't know, but I'll find a way!"

"I know you're honest," the smiling GI said. "I'll let you take them in the mail sacks, and you can just drag them through the corridor to the door, one at a time, and return the sacks later."

"Thank you." Elisabeth smiled and bent her back to the task. Only two doors in that large Palace of Justice were opened to the street. All others were kept locked for security reasons. After dragging the mail bags to the door, she still had a problem.

"Now how do I get them from here to the home of the conference president?" she wondered. "If I call a Jeep, I can put one bag in the back and I can ride in front with the driver. That would take six trips. A command car could probably carry two bags." Like a flash came the thought, "Call a weapons carrier."

"That's it," she said to herself and set off to call the motor pool. "Do you have a weapons carrier avaliable?"

"Yes," came the reply. "Who wants it and for what purpose?"

"Just send it to Miss Redelstein in Room 113 at the courthouse, please." Shortly the weapons carrier arrived, and all six bags of Bibles were loaded aboard. "The best weapons this vehicle ever carried!" Elisabeth chuckled. "Six bags full of two-edged swords."

The conference president walked round and round the boxes of Bibles as they were unloaded at his office. "I can't believe it! I can't believe it!" he kept repeating over and over. "Praise the Lord! Praise the Lord!"

3
From Ochsenhausen to Johnstown

Elisabeth had grown up in the strict religious atmosphere of a Catholic home. As a girl her fondest ambition had been to become a nun, and the two years she spent in a convent boarding school deepened that desire. The autumn she was fifteen, however, found her back at home in Ochsenhausen with her stern father—the town mayor—and her fun-loving mother and four brothers. But Elisabeth was not happy.

For a long time she had been aware of the incompatability between her parents. The crisis came that autumn when her mother took the two younger boys and went to live in Stuttgart. The two older boys were in boarding school, and Elisabeth stayed at home with her father and a housekeeper while she attended business college.

As faithful members of the church, her parents obtained a legal separation rather than a divorce. It was bad enough to have her mother leave home, but when after nearly a year Elisabeth visited her in Stuttgart, she learned something that made her even more sad. Her mother took her to a religious meeting conducted by members of an American sect. A sect which didn't even have a church to meet in, only a hired hall. Then her mother told her the story.

One day after she had been in Stuttgart about half a year, a young man came to the door, handing out religious tracts. When she saw the tract, she said, "I have my own church, and I get my religious literature from my church."

"But, Madam, this tract has new light for the present age."

"Oh," Mother said, "I'm always looking for new light. You may leave the tract." She read it and was so impressed that she shared it with her friend across the hall.

"Look," her friend said, "on the back there's a notice about some Bible lectures being given in the city. Why don't we go and see what they're all about? If they're as good as this tract, they ought to be all right for us to attend."

At the front of the lecture hall were pictures of ferocious-looking beasts, which the speaker said represented world empires as depicted in Bible prophecy. One of those wild beasts had a "notable little horn," which the preacher said represented the Catholic Church.

"I don't think we should stand for this," Mother whispered to her friend. As soon as the meeting was over, she marched up to the front of the hall and confronted the speaker. "You have no right to talk about the church like that. It's an insult to the people who come to listen to you."

"I'm sorry if I offended you," the preacher apologized, "but if you'll bring your Bible and come next week, I'm sure you'll find that everything we say is right in your own Bible. Or, if you like, I'll come to your home and study with you personally."

In spite of misgivings, Mother and her friend attended the meetings every week and even had studies in their own homes. The more they studied the clearer the Bible became.

"Although I've been a faithful member of the church all my life," her mother told Elisabeth, "I knew very little about the Bible. I discovered that this man could not only preach about wild beasts and the world empires of history, but he also knew how to make God come alive as a loving Father. For the first time in my life I grasped the Bible truth that Jesus Christ is truly the only means of salvation, the only Intercessor between humanity and God. I'd always thought of God and Christ as deities entitled to reverence and fear. But now God is a personal friend. I love Him and want to obey Him."

Elisabeth went home from that visit a very depressed young

woman, for she knew that her mother was going to be baptized and join the Seventh-day Adventist Church.

Not many months later joy and disappointment battled inside Elisabeth. Mother was coming home, and her heart thrilled to the news. But she cringed every time she thought about her mother rejecting the true church. Elisabeth felt that her mother had disgraced the family. She determined to win her back to the faith.

Purchasing a Catholic Bible, she studied diligently to show her mother the error of her way. She and her mother had long, earnest discussions about the Bible and religion. Patiently, kindly, her mother told her of God's love, of Christ's sacrifice, of His ministry in heaven, of His coming again, of the resurrection of the righteous at His coming, of the final destruction of the wicked. Her mother explained that the wicked would be "burned up root and branch," not to burn continually.

In vain Elisabeth searched her Bible for evidence to counteract these teachings. But in spite of herself, she began to see that her mother was telling her the truth and showing her the only way of salvation.

Now the obedience Elisabeth had learned at home and at the convent school stared her straight in the face. If she loved God and accepted Jesus as her Saviour and Lord and believed the Bible to be His Word, and if the Bible told her that the seventh day is the Sabbath, then she would be denying her love for Him if she did not keep the Sabbath—keep it in commemoration of His great creation and of His new creation in her life.

If Jesus is the only Intercessor between God and man, then how could she go to a priest and confess her sins and expect him to intercede for her?

Besides her own corrected conscience, Elisabeth was aware of the great change in her mother. Ever since her parents had reunited, Elisabeth and the other family members remarked that Mother was a brand-new person. She was sweet and patient under all circumstances. Even Elisabeth's father began to soften under her gentle influence. However, he bitterly opposed Adventism and refused to let her discuss religion with him.

The Thursday before Easter, 1909, as her father was leaving for his office, he stopped in the kitchen and asked Elisabeth, "Have you been to confession today?"

"No, Father," she replied with trembling, "I haven't been to confession, and I don't think I'll ever go again."

"What?" he shouted, instantly in a rage. "Let me tell you something. It's bad enough for your mother to do what she did, but I will never tolerate one of my children leaving the church. Now this is Holy Thursday; you go to confession this afternoon and behave yourself like a good Catholic, or there will be no room for you under this roof!" With that he slammed the door and was gone.

Trembling, Elisabeth went to her room, fell on her knees and prayed for wisdom and strength. Then she went out to the garden where her mother was planning the planting of spring flowers.

When Elisabeth told her what had happened, her mother said, "Well, child, you don't eat soup as hot as it is dished up. You let it cool off a bit. You wait awhile, and I'll talk to him and everything will be all right."

But all her mother's powers of persuasion failed. Before long it was clear that Elisabeth would have to drop out of school and get a job. She answered a newspaper ad and secured a job in the city of Ulm, working in a lawyer's home.

She was more or less a nanny, helping care for the three children—William, 13; Irene, 12; and Gretel, 10. She was now 17, not much older than the children she looked after. She did not work Saturdays. She went to church every week in an upstairs room over a carpenter's shop. That summer she was baptized in the public bath house.

After nine months Elisabeth began thinking about her future. She decided to go to school and study to be a teacher. Going home, she asked her father for money to attend the Adventist school at Friedensau.

"Not one red penny of my money goes to the Adventists!" He slammed his fist down on the table.

"Father, you know I have my own money that Grandmother left me. You don't have to give me any of your money."

"Huh! You're not of age. I control that money. So just forget about going to an Adventist school. Go anywhere else you want, and I'll give you some money."

Elisabeth applied at the Froebel Training School in Berlin and was accepted. When she went to enroll, however, and told the head mistress that she wanted to be excused from Saturday classes because she was a Seventh-day Adventist, the mistress threw up her hands.

"Whoever heard of such a thing?" she exclaimed. "I'm a good Christian, but I go to church only once a month. People who go to church so often become religious fanatics. Besides, you have two hours of classwork on Saturday."

Suddenly Elisabeth remembered something she'd heard about this woman—that she was out to make every cent of money she could. And so Elisabeth said, "Frau Krohman, if I keep track of all the Saturdays I miss and make them up afterwards, how would that be?"

Immediately the woman saw the point. If Elisabeth made up the Sabbaths for the entire course, she would have to stay several weeks longer, and that would mean more money from her.

"Oh, that can be arranged," she beamed. "That will be all right."

Elisabeth finished the year's course and got her diploma. She had no trouble passing the examinations even though she had missed Sabbath classes. But she still had to stay around the school to make up those missed Sabbaths. During this time an American woman, Mrs. Waters, came to the school looking for a governess to teach her daughters German. Elisabeth got the job. She became governess to Betty, 10, and Petie, 8.

Mrs. Waters, her sister, and the girls were staying at a beautiful boarding hotel. Every day Elisabeth went there to tutor the children. Mrs. Waters treated her courteously.

One day when Elisabeth came, Mrs. Waters said, "We're going to take a few weeks at the seashore. Can you come along?"

"Can I?" Elisabeth's heart beat faster. She was nineteen, and this would be her first trip to the seashore.

The days passed. Elisabeth and the girls enjoyed the seashore with its pounding surf and misty horizon. Then suddenly one afternoon Betty's appendix flared up.

Mrs. Waters cabled her husband, who flew over from America to take his family home.

"We don't want Betty operated on here," Mr. Waters explained to Elisabeth. "So we're taking her back to the States. But we'd like you to accompany us to America. We want you to continue as governess to our girls."

Mrs. Waters smiled. "Fräulein, we'd like you to sign a two-year contract. At the end of that time we'll pay your way back to Germany."

Elisabeth wasn't sure what she should do. She wrote to her mother for advice. "It's a wonderful opportunity for you," her mother wrote back. "Go ahead, and I'm sure God will go with you."

So Elisabeth went to America. They landed in New York on Friday, October 13, 1911. From there they took a train for Johnstown, Pennsylvania. The Waters home was located on the outskirts of Johnstown. It wasn't long before Elisabeth became a regular part of the household.

Years later, she was able to look back and say, "Life in the lap of luxury wasn't always soft and comfortable. Betty and Petie were mischievous youngsters, and sometimes downright naughty. In Germany we got along beautifully because they were dependent on me for everything. But in America I was the stranger, and they were at home. I supervised the study period of their regular school lessons as well as teaching them German. Sometimes they didn't want to study; and when I would say, 'Petie, it is time to study your arithmetic lesson,' she would toss her curls and say, 'I don't have to if I don't want to.'

"Betty had a violent temper and would throw herself on the floor in a tantrum, kicking her heels against the floor in machine-gun fashion. Because of a weak heart, Mrs. Waters had to lead a calm life, but she told me if the children did not mind me I was to tell her. When they had tried my patience to the limit, I would threaten to tell their mother. 'Yes,' would be the saucy reply, 'you can go tell Mother. You don't care if she has a heart attack because she isn't your mother!"

Evidently Mr. and Mrs. Waters realized what a difficult time Elisabeth was having with the girls. Mrs. Waters went out of her way to be kind and cheerful. She bought Elisabeth many fine clothes besides paying her wages.

Mr. and Mrs. Waters took Elisabeth on trips with them and generally encouraged her to stay on as the girls' governess.

Before too many months rolled past, Elisabeth was talking, reading, and writing English with ease.

4
New Horizons

One Sabbath early in 1913 when she returned from church Elisabeth said, "Mrs. Waters, there's going to be a big meeting, a General Conference session of our church, at Washington, D.C., this spring. Delegates from many parts of the world and even Germany will be there. I'd like very much to attend. It may be a once-in-a-lifetime opportunity for me to go and meet the leaders of our church work. Would it be all right with you if I plan to go?"

"Of course, Fräulein," Mrs. Waters answered. "I'm sure we can cope with the girls for a week or so. It will be a wonderful opportunity for you to see our nation's capital. That will be an education in itself."

Elisabeth arrived in Washington in May. The General Conference was held in Takoma Park, Maryland, a suburb of Washington. There she found the big tent pitched on the campus of the Foreign Missionary Seminary (later to become Washington Missionary College, and now Columbia Union College).

The sermons thrilled Elisabeth. She enjoyed the reports and mission stories. But what attracted her most were the stories of China told by Harry Miller and Elder I. H. Evans. She'd heard how Dr. Miller had gone out to China as a pioneer missionary in 1903 and how he dressed like the Chinese, even to wearing the "pigtail." As she sat with her girl friend near the front of the tent one evening listening to his recital of the great spiritual and physical needs of the Chinese people, she said, "I am going to go to China as a missionary."

"You? What do you think you would do in China?" her friend asked.

"I don't know, but I've just decided that I'm going to go to school so that I can be a missionary."

Her decision remained in her mind when she returned to Johnstown. She completed her two-year contract with the Waters family and even stayed on for another year. Then in the fall of 1914 she enrolled at the Clinton Theological Seminary in Clinton, Missouri. For three years she worked hard earning her board and room by housework and teaching church school. She studied just as diligently as she worked. During those three years she was completely cut off from her homeland because World War I severed all connections with Germany. She felt the brunt of American hatred toward Germans during those years. But every summer she relaxed with her American family in Johnstown and watched her naughty little charges grow into young women.

During these three trying years, Elisabeth saw God's guiding hand in every experience, but at no time more clearly than in the summer of 1916. She and a friend volunteered for the literature ministry that summer and were assigned to work in Kansas. Before they left, however, a flood swept through that area, and so their trip was canceled. They went instead to Saint Louis to help with an evangelistic effort and to sell magazines on the street.

Her friend sold many magazines, but Elisabeth scarcely earned "the salt for her soup."

Her Bible instructor said, "Elisabeth, don't get discouraged. If we don't get word from the school that your name is on the list of students working for a scholarship, perhaps God has something else for you to do." Elisabeth and her teacher set a date by which they would know whether or not she was to continue with her magazines. The word did not come by the specified date. Disappointed, Elisabeth quit trying to sell magazines and began working in the home of a wealthy businessman.

In this home Elisabeth became friends with the Hungarian Catholic cook. The common bond of their language in a foreign country drew them together.

The cook did Elisabeth's work on Saturday so she could have Sabbath off, and Elisabeth worked for her on Sunday. As the days went by, the cook asked Elisabeth many questions about her faith and her way of life. Little by little, Elisabeth unfolded the basis and the substance of her faith. The cook seemed genuinely interested.

Mrs. Waters, however, thought Elisabeth should come home to Johnstown for summer vacation as she had done before, and upon her urging, Elisabeth decided to go. When she told the cook that she was leaving, the young woman cried, "I've just begun to get a glimpse of something better than I've ever known before, and now you go and leave me."

"I'll get someone to come and really study the Bible with you," Elisabeth told her. Before she left for Johnstown, Elisabeth introduced the cook to the area Bible worker.

"I used to wonder when Elisabeth first came to the house what that black book was that she was always reading," the cook said. "And so one day when she was away, I peeked to see and discovered that it was the Holy Bible. I was curious to know what there was about it that was so interesting." The Bible worker immediately scheduled Bible studies.

It was a happy day for Elisabeth when she learned that the cook had been baptized. Later, when the cook left, the girl who replaced her studied with the Bible worker, and she, too, was baptized.

"God had a special plan for me that summer," Elisabeth said, when she heard the news. "He shaped circumstances so that I'd be at the right place at the right time. Two people were converted and became workers in His cause because I quit selling magazines and went to work for that businessman."

The next summer, back in Johnstown after graduation, Elisabeth began to think about taking nurses' training as a preparation for mission service.

Mrs. Waters encouraged her, and in the autumn of 1918 she was accepted for the nursing school at the Washington Sanitarium. At last she was headed down the road to her life's career. Freshmen nursing students, the "probies," were expected to do all the cleaning work—everything from working in the kitchen to cleaning rooms, washing windows, and mopping floors.

"Well, this is all good training for a would-be missionary," Elisabeth thought. She tackled without complaining any job assigned her. Because of her willingness, more and more difficult jobs came her way.

"When will I study?" she wondered. Early in the morning would be the best time, she decided. But before long the matron noticed she was an early riser and said, "I think you'd be a good one to mop the sanitarium halls first thing in the morning before the staff comes on for day duty."

The matron rolled out the "mop wagon" and showed her how to use it. "You'll notice," she explained, "that one side of the bucket contains soapy water for the first mopping, and the other side has clear for the second mopping. And this is the way the wringer works." She demonstrated.

All went well until Elisabeth was ready to go downstairs. As she started pushing the awkward contraption through the elevator door, one wheel jammed. Before she could joggle it loose, the "wagon" toppled over and water poured down the elevator shaft!

Weeks passed. Elisabeth was delighted to have the great China Doctor, Dr. Miller, as one of her instructors. He was medical superintendent of the institution at that time.

During the flu epidemic of the winter of 1918, the sanitarium was crowded with patients. Elisabeth was the first nursing student to surrender to the "bug." Her strenuous program had weakened her, and she had already lost considerable weight.

The doctors didn't know much about influenza, and about as soon as a patient's fever subsided, he was sent home, to make room for another patient. And so it was with Elisabeth. Dr.

Miller, himself, put her in a wheelchair and wheeled her to the nurses' dormitory. After another day or two, she was back on duty.

Within a few more days, however, she was back in the sanitarium, seriously ill with inflammation of the kidneys. There she lay in bed for four weeks, learning what it is like to be a patient instead of a nurse. "A valuable experience for any nurse or doctor," she declared later.

By the time she was able to be released again, she thought she'd better go home to Johnstown to recuperate. "If you go home now," Dr. Miller counseled, "they'll never let you come back when they see how much weight you've lost and how weak your heart is as a result of the high fever."

"But how will I ever make up seven weeks of classwork? I might as well drop out and start over again next year."

"Oh, you'll make it up somehow. You just write to your family and tell them that you're getting well. Then you stay on here and get some rest and don't do any physical work for a while."

Until she was stronger, her fellow students pushed her to classes in a wheelchair, and she spent all the time her strength would allow in study.

That first year was difficult, not only because of the hard work and illness, but Elisabeth still felt that she was an alien. Some people seemed to delight in talking about those "terrible Germans" in her presence.

She never attended the programs, entertainments, and parties arranged for the students. How could she laugh and have fun when she didn't know what had happened to her family in Germany? She spent her Saturday nights alone in her room studying.

Elisabeth's summer was spent with the Waters family. That American family, which considered her a member, replenished her wardrobe and buoyed up her spirits. After three restful months with them, she was back in Washington for her second year of training.

November 11, 1918, was a day of jubilation in Washington—

the Armistice had been signed! Gradually the cutting remarks about the Germans died down, and Elisabeth felt more at ease. But her heart was still heavy, wondering whether her brothers had been in the war, whether any of them had been killed, whether their home was still standing. Finally, letters came. One from her parents and one from her brother Walter.

Elisabeth held them, afraid to open them. After many hesitating minutes, she tore them open. And when she did she learned that at least part of her fears had been well grounded. Two brothers, the oldest and the youngest, had been killed in the war. But the rest of her family were safe.

Dr. H. G. Hadley operated a clinic in the ghetto section of Washington. All third-year nursing students from the sanitarium spent three months at the clinic. Here they learned to care for patients suffering with diseases that seldom showed up at the sanitarium. The sanitarium clientele consisted mostly of well-to-do people, many of them from the Government personnel in Washington, and others from far away.

In the clinic the nurses had to do everything from cleaning to firing the furnace. Firing that old furnace was the bane of the nurses. Time and again the fire would go out and the building grow cold. Then Elisabeth would have to go down and start the fire again and bank it for the night. The next day it was someone else's turn to fire the furnace, and the same thing happened all over again.

One cold day Elisabeth said, "Look, girls, I know how to fire a furnace and keep the fire going. Why don't you let me do it and make that my special job? I'd rather do it from the beginning than to have to clean out the grates after you've made a mess of things."

"Oh, would you?" the other nursing students exclaimed. "Oh, Elisabeth, we'd love you for that." And so she became the furnace tender. She had learned this skill from Mr. Waters, who, as president of the National Radiator Corporation, insisted that every member of his household know how to fire a furnace and bank a fire.

To this point in her nurses' training, Elisabeth had never seen a delivery. Now at the clinic many babies were born. And Doctor Hadley often made house calls to deliver babies. Elisabeth stayed five months at the clinic, instead of the usual three. During that time she assisted with twenty-five deliveries, twelve of which she managed by herself.

When graduation came, Elisabeth had not yet made up all the work she'd missed in her freshman year. So she was still in stripes when her classmates wore their new white uniforms. Nevertheless, she was asked to be assistant to the Director of Nurses, and in that position she finished her senior year.

In the fall of 1921 it was time for Elisabeth and her classmates to take state board examinations in order to be certified as registered nurses. "Examination!" she trembled at the thought. Although she read and spoke the English language very well, the thought of taking an examination in English petrified her. She decided she would not fill out the application blanks.

When Dr. Miller heard about it, he marched right over to the dormitory. "What is this I hear," he demanded, "about your not sending in the application to take state boards?"

"Dr. Miller, I've never failed at anything in my whole life, but I feel very insecure about this," she said. "Rather than fail, I decided not to take the examination."

"Ridiculous!" he said. "Here, fill out these blanks right away." He thrust the blanks into her hands. "You're going to take state boards. I'll take the blanks to the notary and have them stamped, and mail them tonight, otherwise it will be too late."

She'd been taking orders from Dr. Miller for three years. When he ordered her to fill out the application, she did. Together they went to the notary's office, and the blanks were soon on their way to Baltimore.

Trembling with fear, Elisabeth went with the others to Baltimore. But when she sat at the desk with those examination papers before her, a sense of calm and assurance steadied her hand, and she began to write. She had asked God's help, and the answer came just when she needed it. When grades were released, and she learned that she had passed in every subject, she declared, "I could never have done it without God's help."

As a new graduate nurse Elisabeth was hired to be head nurse in the sanitarium. She was put in charge of the eye, nose, and throat department. She loved the job and thrilled at really earning money for her work.

The Washington Sanitarium grew during these years. It expanded, by enlarging the annex to sixty-five beds. The annex was a three-floor facility, with surgical patients on top floor, medical patients on second floor, and sanitarium-type patients on first. Dr. Miller asked Elisabeth if she would supervise the annex.

"Oh, Dr. Miller, I could never do that–sixty-five beds and treatment rooms!" she said. "I could never handle that. It is too much responsibility."

"Yes, you can," he replied confidently. "I've got to go to China. They've asked me to go over and help choose land where we can build a sanitarium in Shanghai. We must have someone to fill in here while I am gone. If you'll do it just while I'm gone, my mind will be at rest on that score. Then when I come back, if you insist, I'll try to find someone else."

When Dr. Miller returned from China, he stopped by the annex to see Elisabeth. After looking around, he told the now confident nurse, "I knew you could do it."

"I could never have done it without the Lord's help," she replied.

Dr. Miller was always springing surprises on Elisabeth. His next surprise came in 1923, when he asked her to become director of nurses. Again she protested, "Dr. Miller, I, German, and only a few years of experience! Surely you can find someone with more experience who could do that job better."

"I've interviewed every department head, and they're all willing to cooperate with you," he said. "And the board has voted it. We think some of your German qualities are just what we need!"

By all these changes, Elisabeth was learning the fine art of adaptability. W. A. Spicer once listed the three most important qualifications for a missionary as "1. Adaptability; 2. Adaptability; 3. Adaptability."

By this time Elisabeth had received her American citizenship.

During that last year Elisabeth met a young man who had been shell-shocked during the war and was now in the employ of the United States Government. Dr. D. H. Kress had treated the man and, in his loving way, ministered to his spiritual needs as well as his physical needs. Before leaving the sanitarium, Ernest Mayo was baptized and joined the church. Even after being dismissed as a patient, he visited the sanitarium often, especially to see some of the nurses. Soon it was one particular nurse—Elisabeth. When he proposed marriage, however, she wasn't sure whether this was God's will for her life. She talked to Dr. Kress about their friendship and asked whether he thought she should marry Ernest Mayo.

"I think it's wonderful," Dr. Kress told her. "Mayo is a fine fellow. But I have great confidence in my wife's judgment. Why don't you talk to her? I won't tell her that I have talked to you."

Dr. Kress's wife was also a doctor, and even more enthusiastic than her husband. "I'm sure it's God's will for you," she told Elisabeth, who now felt confident that she could follow her heart. The next day she gave Ernest Mayo an affirmative answer.

She decided that the fall of 1924 was the time to visit her family in Germany. She had come to America for two years but had stayed thirteen. She planned to leave as soon as graduation was over.

Shortly before graduation, however, her cousin, a nursery governess for a family in New York phoned her. "You know we are going to Europe," she told Elisabeth. "But the nurse who was to go with us can't go now. Couldn't you come along as nurse for the children? You'd get all your expenses paid and your wages as nurse besides."

"That's too good an offer to turn down!" Elisabeth's heart pounded at the thought. "I'll really try to work into your plans."

"Go before graduation?" Dr. Miller asked incredulously when she mentioned the subject. "You wouldn't want to disappoint the students, would you?"

"Dr. Miller, it means over five hundred dollars, and I don't have much money," she insisted. "Furthermore, it is a large class this year, and I've already signed the diplomas. All applications for state board are made out. I can easily turn things over to someone else."

"All right. I'll take it up at faculty meeting this afternoon," the doctor promised.

When Mayo learned that she was going to Germany, he urged her to marry him, and they would take their honeymoon in Europe. "No," Elisabeth said, "I want to go home for the first time after such a long absence as my parents' daughter and not as your wife."

Soon everything was settled, and a happy Elisabeth headed for home. The family she traveled with provided wonderful accommodations on the big French liner. She enjoyed taking care of the two darling babies, crooning and cuddling them and watching their bright eyes fill with wonder. For a week they stayed in a palatial hotel in Paris. While there, Elisabeth found more than one opportunity for sightseeing.

And then it was home to Ochsenhausen and a long-awaited reunion with her family. Her father had now decided that she could amount to something, even if she were a member of the Seventh-day Adventist Church. He never apologized for having driven her away from home, but he treated her like any other family member.

When she told her family that she was engaged, her mother was thrilled and even her father seemed pleased. He gave her money to buy her trousseau, and she and her mother spent many hours shopping and sewing.

A few weeks later Mayo wrote that he was being sent to

Brussels to work in the United States Embassy there. He came to Ochsenhausen and met Elisabeth's family. He and Elisabeth planned a spring wedding.

However, at Brussels one obstacle after another blocked the way for carrying out their plans. For one thing, he had to get his birth certificate from his home state of Kentucky. It didn't come and didn't come. He urged Elisabeth to come to Brussels, and they would be married there. She took her trousseau and went. Weeks went by and more and more obstacles popped up.

In the meantime, Mayo became irritable, and his association at the Embassy led him back into many non-Christian ways. He did not seem the same man Elisabeth had known in America. His erratic behavior made her wonder if he still suffered some of the effects of shell-shock. In distress, she wrote to her parents.

Her father replied, "You'd better come home. I'd rather set fire to your trousseau than to have you marry someone you could not be happy with."

Elisabeth prayed and prayed about it. Finally she concluded that all the obstacles must be God's way of trying to prevent a mistake that might ruin her life. "If you'd acted like this in America," she told Mayo, "I never would have consented to marry you." Against his violent protests, she packed up and went home to Ochsenhausen.

In the spring, about the time she was to have been married, she boarded a ship for America. Who should she find as a fellow passenger, but Dr. Miller. As full of surprises as always, the doctor told Elisabeth, "Don't accept any work in America when you get back. I'm going to China, and I want you to come out and be in charge of our nurses' training school."

5

China at Last

The General Conference told Dr. Miller that Elisabeth could not go to China. "There's no budget for another nurse," they said.

"Well, keep it in mind," the doctor pleaded, "and see that she's sent out just as soon as funds are available. How can I organize and operate a sanitarium-hospital in Shanghai if I don't have experienced help?"

"You have a long way to go yet before the hospital is finished," the committee said. "Maybe funds will be available by that time."

Dr. Miller returned to China alone.

At her American home in Johnstown, Elisabeth prepared for China. But when she learned that no funds were available, she said to Mrs. Waters, "I think I'd better look for work somewhere."

"Fräulein, you know Betty is expecting her first baby. Couldn't you go and stay with her for several weeks to help during her confinement and afterward? She'll be at the lying-in hospital in Chicago. I'd appreciate your going, since my heart condition prohibits my being there."

"I'll be glad to go," Elisabeth said. "Not only for Betty's sake, but it will give me opportunity to observe and maybe do some work in the maternity ward. It's one of the best-known maternity centers in America, you know."

A few months later Elisabeth performed a like service for Betty's cousin at the Elisabeth Steel McGee Hospital in

Pittsburgh. Elisabeth stayed on at the hospital to work for several weeks.

"Now Petie is going to have a baby," Mrs. Waters announced one day. "I hope you can hold your schedule open to take care of her when the time comes."

"Petie!" Visions of the naughty little girl tossing her curls, stamping her foot, and saying, "I don't have to if I don't want to," flashed through Elisabeth's mind, but she went to Columbus, Ohio, and took care of Petie and her baby.

With vacations at home between these special cases, the months rolled by until the spring of 1927. The daily newspapers carried news of trouble in China. Elisabeth wondered what the outcome would be and how it would affect her. "This word about all the foreigners in interior China rushing to the port cities doesn't sound good," she commented to Mr. and Mrs. Waters. Next came word that the General Conference was recalling all missionaries from China whose furloughs would fall due within the next year.

"I just can't sit around waiting to go to China when people are coming home," she said. "I think I'll write to that big hospital in Philadelphia and apply for some special training in maternity work."

"With all the experience you have already had in that line," Mrs. Waters said laughingly, "you'll be a real professional if you take any more training."

"That's what I want. I'll send my application right away."

She sat down at the desk in her room ready to write for a job when she heard the telephone ring.

"It's for you, Fräulein. Washington calling."

"Hello," Elisabeth said.

"Get ready to go to China as soon as you can," the General Conference Secretary on the other end said.

"Why," Elisabeth stammered, "I thought people were coming home and that you weren't sending out anyone now. What about the budget? Are funds available?"

"People are coming home all right, and we don't have a

budget, but Dr. Miller is urging us to send you out. He thinks the situation will clear up before long, and he says in the meantime you can study the language."

Elisabeth's mind spun with the news. She was going to head out for China!

"You'll be interested to know," the voice went on, "that when Elder I. H. Evans passed through Hawaii, he met a man from California. This man asked Elder Evans if there was some particular need in China to which he could contribute money without going through regular channels.

" 'Yes,' Elder Evans told him, 'we have a nurse under appointment, but there's no budget to pay her salary.'

" 'That's a good project. I'll pay her transportation and her salary for one year,' the man said. So there you are, Miss Redelstein, the Lord has opened the way for you to go forward. We'll secure passports and visas for you here in Washington. We'd like you to sail the latter part of May."

"Thank You, Lord," Elisabeth prayed as she hung up. "Now I know You want me in China. I can go forward confidently, fearing nothing in spite of China's problems. Thank You, Lord."

Elisabeth arrived in Shanghai in the middle of June, 1927. She found the city in a state of jitters. General Chiang Kai-shek was trying to organize a strong central government. The age-old system of war lords stood in his way. Before anything significant could be accomplished, this system had to be abolished. No war lord wanted to give up authority over his province. If at all possible he wanted to extend his rule over neighboring provinces. In their efforts to resist the general's march from the south to the north, the war lords often fought with one another.

Somehow foreigners symbolized the cause of their trouble. "Oust the Foreign Devils" became the battle cry in many interior places. The war lords' atrocities, or the rumors of such things, sent most foreigners scampering for the port cities.

Every home in the China Division compound on Ningkuo

Road overflowed with women and children who had left the interior mission stations. Many of these women used this waiting period to study the language. The Shanghai Language School, presided over by William A. Scharffenberg, provided teachers for the women. Elisabeth arrived on Thursday, and Sunday morning she began language study.

Having already mastered French and English, Elisabeth found the Chinese language less difficult to learn than did others who knew only English. She completed the full one-year's course of study in three quarters and was ready to go to work.

The political situation quieted down, and the new sanitarium-hospital opened its doors for business in February, 1928. "You'll never fill up that white elephant, away out there in the country, twelve miles from the city!" the people predicted. "The wealthy can have doctors come to their homes, and the poor can't afford it."

Dr. Miller's blue eyes twinkled in his round, rosy-cheeked face, but he said nothing. He looked like a Chinese sage who knew a secret he could not share. Within six months sixty-five patients filled the fifty-bed hospital to overflowing. Not only Chinese but many Americans as well utilized the hospital facilities. Missionaries of all faiths appreciated the hospital.

A Methodist lady, when Elisabeth apologized for having to put another bed in her room, said, "I don't care. Put in a third bed if necessary, and we'll call it the Methodist Ward. It's wonderful to have a hospital where we can be cared for without having to go home to the States."

A few days later Elisabeth looked at the group of young men and women, little more than boys and girls, who presented themselves before her as candidates for the nurses' training course. Most of them understood no English, and were unfamiliar with all the foreign objects in the hospital including a foreign-style bed with a mattress.

"They'll have to learn the English names of the most ordinary things," Elisabeth decided. So she taught a class in English every day. At the same time, she showed them how to take temperatures, give baths, and make beds. Although eager to learn, the students found English as difficult as the Americans found Chinese.

In class one day a girl asked, "Why do we have to go so fast before an operation?"

"I don't know anything about having to go fast before an operation," Elisabeth said, wondering what the girl was talking about.

"It says in the book something about a fast before an operation."

"Oh!" Elisabeth laughed. "*Fast* in that case means abstinence from food."

The Chinese language also has words that sound the same but have different meanings. In Chinese, however, the word is said with a different inflection of the voice for each meaning. The Chinese teachers loved to tell stories about the mistakes foreigners made by not using the right tone. One of their favorite stories was about an American who sent his servant to the market to bring home a chicken, and the servant came bringing a wife for the man.

Every day brought new problems and new joys to Elisabeth. One student, practicing taking temperatures, declared, "This thermometer no good!"

Elisabeth looked at the thermometer. "It looks all right to me. Let me see you use it." She watched as the student nurse took the thermometer in her hand by the mercury end and stuck the other end in the "patient's" mouth.

"I thought this end handle," the embarrassed girl giggled when shown the proper way to use it.

"Don't be embarrassed," Elisabeth said. "When I was in college, I once tried sterilizing a thermometer by pouring boiling water over it." The whole class tittered. Elisabeth felt the tension lessen.

Much as she loved her students, Elisabeth Redelstein longed for some more trained nurses. Mr. and Mrs. O. G. Erich were the only two other foreign nurses on the staff. Mrs. Erich was in charge of the women's hydrotherapy. Mr. Erich had charge of the X-ray department as well as supervising the men's hydrotherapy. Mrs. Paul, wife of Dr. Paul, was in charge of the dispensary in the city, but she also served as operating room nurse when necessary. Only student nurses were available for private-duty nursing, and they required close supervision. Consequently, Elisabeth was on duty in the hospital practically day and night.

Dr. Miller's reputation as a goiter specialist spread, and patients came from as far away as the Philippines. "This is a very serious case," the doctor explained to Elisabeth about one Filipino patient. "I can't trust her to student nurses. I'll stay with her in the evenings until eleven o'clock; then if you can come on and stay with her until morning, we can special her through the night. Your advanced students can look after her in the daytime with your supervision."

Later, after a trip to Manila, the doctor told Elisabeth about another special case. "I found a male patient in Manila who has a very bad goiter that should be removed. But he also has a very bad heart, which makes surgery a risk. I can't operate on him down there, because he'll need special care after surgery, and I can't stay down there to nurse him."

The man's family arranged to have him come to Shanghai. An ambulance met the patient at the boat and conveyed him to the sanitarium, and Dr. Miller operated. Knowing how concerned the doctor was about this case, Elisabeth watched the patient with extra care after the doctor returned to his home on the other side of the city.

She had worked with Dr. Miller on so many goiter cases that she knew what to expect. Noticing that the patient's pulse and temperature were different from any other goiter case she'd ever seen, she called the on-duty doctor. He removed the blood-soaked dressing, cleaned the incision area, and put on clean dressings.

Not long afterward, Elisabeth noticed again this disturbing relationship between pulse and temperature. Again she called the doctor. He came and looked at the dressings.

"There's no sign of bleeding," he said. "I've changed the dressings. I think you're unduly concerned. The patient seems to me to be getting along all right."

Still unsatisfied, Elisabeth waited until she heard the on-duty doctor drive away. Then she hurried to the telephone and called Dr. Miller. "Doctor, there's something wrong with this goiter patient," she said.

"I'll be right out." The phone clicked. Dr. Miller had a reputation of driving recklessly. Shanghai streets thronged with slow-moving pedestrians, hundreds of bicycles, rickshaws, coolies carrying huge loads bouncing up and down at either end of a bamboo pole across their shoulders. Other coolies pushed and pulled wagons of lumber or iron pipes, and ancient automobiles honked for the right of way. The right of way belonged to the loudest and most persistent honker. Dr. Miller must have kept his hand on the horn all the way from his house to the hospital, for he arrived in an unbelievably short time.

Elisabeth heard his short, quick steps hurrying down the hall. As he entered the patient's room she handed him the chart. He looked at it, and moved over to the bed. For a moment he bent over the patient.

"He's bleeding inside. We'll have to open the wound." Soon the patient was in the operating room, where Dr. Miller opened the wound, cleaned out the area, sutured the bleeding vessels, and put on fresh dressings. Elisabeth assisted at every step of the procedure.

With the patient back in his room, the doctor said, "I'll stay with him now for a while. You get some rest."

She headed for home. At the hospital door she looked back and saw the doctor standing by the patient's bed with a glass of orange juice fortified with dextrose in his hand. His other hand and arm supported the patient's head while he poured juice down the man's throat. "We have to get some nourishment down you," he was saying to the patient.

At nine o'clock that evening, Elisabeth, alone in her room at the sanitarium, heard a rap on the door. Opening it, she found Dr. Miller standing there, nervously stroking his hair. "Miss Redelstein," he said, "I want to tell you how grateful I am that we have someone who is watching the patients as closely as you watched that goiter patient. He wouldn't be here now if you hadn't called me."

"I'm just thankful that the Lord saw fit to use me if it helped save someone's life," she said.

Wealthy Chinese and government officials came to the sanitarium, sometimes for illness, sometimes for a rest and physical check-up. They enjoyed the quiet atmosphere of the sanitarium in its rural setting. Many commented on its well-manicured lawns, flower gardens, rows of sweet peas gaily climbing the fence, the spreading Chinese elms, and the Japanese maples. Inside, they appreciated the tasteful blending of Chinese and foreign influence under the artistic hand of Mrs. E. C. Wood. They praised the skill of the physicians and the gentle care of the nurses.

Among those who came to the sanitarium was Madame Chiang Kai-shek's mother. The Madame came to visit her and also to visit other patients from time to time. She showed great interest in the work of the sanitarium, especially the training school.

Often she stopped at Elisabeth's office and asked, "How are things going, Miss Redelstein?" Through these casual contacts a real friendship developed between the wife of the Generalissimo of China and Elisabeth.

More than once Elisabeth enjoyed being a guest for tea in the Madame's beautiful home, where gorgeous Peking rugs in sculptured designs and pleasant colors set off the handsome carved furniture. Here Elisabeth developed an appreciation for Chinese art at its best. Each room in a wealthy Chinese home usually contained one central art object which drew the beholder's interest like a magnet. It might be a picture on the wall, a large vase of flowers, a jade or soapstone carving. No matter what the object, it stood out for its beauty and simplicity.

After two years as director of the training school, supervisor of nursing care, often private-duty nurse and night supervisor, Elisabeth rejoiced to learn that a night supervisor was coming from America. Happily she went with a group of the other missionaries to meet the ship and welcome the new nurse. "She has no idea how welcome she really is," Elisabeth thought as she stood on the wharf. But the new nurse was not on board. Elisabeth felt disappointment almost to the point of despair.

"I just can't go back to the hospital," Elisabeth thought as she walked up and down on the wharf. But she did go back, and for another eight weeks she carried the whole load until Miss Matilda Follett arrived to take over as night supervisor. At last Elisabeth got some rest.

When a Chinese patient left the sanitarium, it was the custom to send a silver shield in appreciation. "We're beginning to look like an armory," Dr. Miller chuckled one day. "We'll have to build a special shield room." Then seriously he added, "I wish we had the money represented by those shields. Why don't we ask these people if they'd be willing to give money to start a hospital in the city for the poor people?"

Three years after the sanitarium opened, the division committee decided to raise money for a hospital in the city. "If we can get $80,000," Dr. Miller estimated, "we can build the first unit of the hospital and be able to take care of at least some patients. Then we can add to it later as funds come in."

When the wealthy former patients were approached about a donation for this cause, they asked, "Is it going to be under the same management? Will the same doctors be serving there?" When assured that this would be the case, they gave so liberally that soon the contributions amounted to $150,000. Former patients were not the only contributors. Merchants in the city gave as well. On Nanking Road, where silk shops and China art shops lined the street, one silk merchant looked at the contribution subscription book and mused, "Ah, ha, I see my competitor across the street has given $10,000. My shop is better than his. I will give $15,000."

Instead of the first unit Dr. Miller had envisioned, the contributions built a complete 180-bed hospital.

A 180-bed hospital and insufficient help! Elisabeth wrote to all the mission directors throughout the Far Eastern Division as well as in China. "If you have any young people interested in taking the nurses' course, send them to Shanghai right away," her letters said. From all parts of China, the students came. And from the Philippines, Japan, Korea, Thailand, Burma, and even some Russian girls from Harbin in Manchuria. Most of these students could not understand English, and those from outside China could not understand Chinese. Undaunted, Elisabeth decided that all courses would be taught double, in Chinese for the Chinese and in English for the foreign students. That class of fifty students learned first-hand a valuable lesson in international relationships. They ate, studied, played, and prayed together.

When in uniform, the students of different nationalities were scarcely distinguishable from one another. But what a picture they made on Sabbath, as dressed in their national costumes they crossed the campus from their dormitory to the charming little high-beamed chapel. These students completed their training and returned to their homelands where many of them helped start training schools in mission hospitals. One young woman from this class, Legaya Reyes, came to America and received her MA degree in nursing education. Today she is in charge of advanced nursing training for Adventist nurses in the Philippines. Two of the nurses from Korea have since received the International Florence Nightingale award.

In 1932 the Japanese invaded Shanghai, setting off another wave of unrest. Because the Chinese felt so strongly against the Japanese, some of the mission staff thought the sanitarium should be closed and the medical staff moved into the new hospital on Range Road in the city. "There'll be trouble at the san," they said. But the Japanese left the sanitarium alone and invaded the Range Road clinic.

Four Japanese soldiers entered the clinic. One stood at each stairway, one at the elevator, and one went up in the elevator. "You are giving signals to the enemy," the officer accused. "We've seen a light going up and down. We know it's a signal to the Chinese."

The clinic manager searched his mind for an answer. "Oh," he said, "what you have seen is the elevator going up and down. You can see the light from outside the building. I assure you that light is not a signal to the Chinese."

The officer looked like he didn't know whether to believe that or not, but his attitude softened somewhat. "You have patients here who have been hurt by the war," he said. "Their relatives may get ugly and shoot at us. You'd better dismiss all the patients who have been hurt by the war."

The staff consulted and decided to tell all ambulatory patients that they should go home. The patients unable to walk were taken by ambulance to the sanitarium.

"There aren't enough beds at the sanitarium for all these people," someone complained.

"That's a small matter," Elisabeth said. "We'll put mattresses on the floor to take care of the overflow."

As the Japanese pressed harder and harder into the city, the Chinese army retreated out past the sanitarium. In morning and evening worship, the staff and students claimed the promise, "The angel of the Lord encampeth round about them that fear him, and delivereth them."

Along the road that led from the city past the sanitarium, Chinese soldiers threw up barbed-wire entanglements and stood guard day and night. As a concession to the hospital staff, they removed the blockade for two hours a day, one hour in the morning and one in late afternoon, so the sanitarium workers could go to the city and return. One evening Elisabeth returned from the city just before the barricade was strung across the road again. When she reached the sanitarium, the nurse in charge told her, "Mrs. Boynton has come in."

"Is Dr. Miller here? Does he know she is here?"

Mr. and Mrs. Allen Boynton, both nurses, had come from

America during the last year. Elisabeth's concern for Mrs. Boynton centered in the fact that her bad heart condition complicated her pregnancy. Elisabeth had often said, "When Mrs. Boynton comes in for delivery, I hope and pray that Dr. Miller will be here."

But now Dr. Miller was not at the sanitarium. He was at his home on Ningkuo Road. "What shall I do?" Elisabeth prayed. Mrs. Boynton's face turned blue at every contraction pain. "The doctor can't come now, the barricade's already across the road for the night." The thought of Peter's deliverance from prison flashed across her mind. "Thank You, Lord, for that thought. If You could send an angel to deliver Peter from prison, You can send an angel to get Dr. Miller through the barricade."

She phoned the doctor. "We'll have the barricade removed for you by the time you get here," she promised. She then found the chaplain, Arthur Mountain. She told him to inform the soldiers that the doctor was coming and not to shoot at him. "You be there with your car," she told Elder Mountain, "so that the doctor can leave his car on the other side and walk past the barricade, and you can pick him up on this side and get him here as soon as possible."

But when an angel undertakes an assignment, he can do it better than that. When Dr. Miller arrived, the soldiers removed the barricade and let him drive through in his own car. The doctor arrived on time. So did the baby. And Mrs. Boynton's life was saved.

Elisabeth's first furlough came in 1932. The father of a little boy named Leslie asked Elisabeth to take the child to Europe with her, so he could stay with relatives in England. Leslie, who had been a patient, was well acquainted with Elisabeth and did not fear going with her.

The first day out from Shanghai the ship's steward came rushing to Elisabeth. "Miss Redelstein, an American woman is about to have a baby. Please come and take care of her. We have no facilities on this boat for such an emergency."

"Get the ship's doctor. I'm only a nurse, and I don't intend to get mixed up in anything like this that might lead to an international incident if something went wrong."

"The doctor doesn't understand English."

"Well, get him on the job anyway, and I'll interpret for him."

The young mother, already three days on the boat from Tientsin, had taken a laxative to relieve her distress, not anticipating in what form the relief would come. The doctor administered some drugs to quiet things down and wired ahead to Hong Kong to have an ambulance meet the boat.

At Hong Kong friends of Elisabeth waited to greet her. "Here, you take care of Leslie," she handed the boy to them. "I have to go to the hospital with a patient." She and the patient raced the stork to the top of the peak. They won, and Elisabeth turned her patient over to the Sisters at Matilda Hospital.

In Manila the sister of the goiter patient whose life Elisabeth had helped save met her at the dock. The woman did everything she could to make Elisabeth's stay in Manila pleasant, taking her shopping and sightseeing. "Your hospital did so much for my brother that I can never repay you," the woman said. Elisabeth spent a month helping organize the training school at the new Manila Sanitarium.

From Manila she and Leslie moved on to Singapore and then to Penang, where she helped work out some problems at the new sanitarium there.

The trip on to Italy and home to Ochsenhausen was without incident. Elisabeth delivered Leslie to an aunt in England and then settled down for six months of rest and recuperation with her loved family and friends.

As a member of the International Nurses Association, Elisabeth received notice of an international convention to be held that summer in Brussels. She went as an American delegate, but when the few German nurses at the convention learned that she was really German, they persuaded her to join their delegation because it was so small.

A happy experience came from this arrangement. The queen of Belgium and one of the German nurses had been roommates at a boarding school when they were young, and so the queen invited her friend and the whole German delegation to come to the palace for tea.

After another three months of visiting her second family and friends in America, it was time to head back for a second term of service in China.

6

Life With Madame Chiang Kai-shek

Back in Shanghai, Elisabeth found that the training school teaching program had not been carried out as she'd planned it. The senior students were way behind in their classwork. Mrs. Letha Coulston, whose husband had died a short time before, was in Shanghai preparing to return to the States.

When Elisabeth talked to her about the desperate need in the training school, Mrs. Coulston said, "I couldn't go and leave you and the young people in need of help. I'll stay and teach in the training school." Mrs. Coulston, trained as both a teacher and a nurse, got the program back on schedule. Between the clinic on Range Road and the sanitarium, the student nurses received a good all-around experience.

While Elisabeth had been on furlough, Dr. Miller had treated many famous patients. None of his cases had more far-reaching effects than did General Chang Hsueh-liang, former ruler of Manchuria and famed "Young Marshal" of the Chinese Republic. The Young Marshal, friend and outstanding field marshal of Chiang Kai-shek, had inherited a fortune and the rulership of Manchuria from his father. A brilliant field commander, General Chang Hsueh-liang put up a strenuous resistance to the Japanese take-over of Manchuria. Though a fighter, and a good one, at heart he was a gentle man. The conflict between his nature and his military role made him easy prey to the opium habit. That habit caused his defeat by the Japanese, and almost destroyed his life.

In 1933 Mr. W. H. Donald, the Young Marshal's advisor from

Australia, persuaded him to come to Shanghai and take "the cure" under Dr. Miller. General Chang Hsueh-liang brought his wife and his second wife, Miss Elsie Chow. They were all addicted to opium. Dr. Miller and his staff patiently took them all through the difficult treatment period. The agonies of withdrawal from opium are so terrible that the patient is often ready to commit murder or suicide.

In appreciation for the cure, the Young Marshal gave Dr. Miller a gift of $50,000. The $50,000 built a hospital in Lanchow, Northwest China. Later the marshal gave more money for the building of the Wuhan Sanitarium just outside the city of Hankow in Central China.

When Madame Chiang Kai-shek learned that Elisabeth was back in Shanghai, she came to see her. "Miss Redelstein, I have a houseboy working for me who is too smart a lad to be doing servant's work," the Madame said. "I'd like to get him into your training school. Are you willing to take him?"

"I'm sorry, but I have all the boys I can handle," Elisabeth replied. "We never need as many male nurses as female, you know. Besides, we don't have a new class starting now."

Several weeks later, the Madame asked again and got about the same answer. This time Elisabeth told Dr. Miller of the Madame's request and her reply.

"Oh, Miss Redelstein," the doctor said, "we can't turn down a request like that. The General and the Madame have been so helpful in ironing out some of our problems. If she makes that request again, you take the boy into the training school and do the very best you can for him."

When it was time to start a new class, the Madame came again with her request. "I'll pay all his expenses," she promised.

"OK," Elisabeth agreed. "Bring the boy in, and he can join the new class." And so the Madame's houseboy came to be trained as a nurse. His name was Han yu-Chu, but Elisabeth called him Caleb—Caleb Chu—just as she gave Bible names to all her students. "I can never keep an alphabetical file on Chinese names," she explained, "with so many of them sounding alike but being spelled differently." She ran out of Bible names for girls and had to resort to such titles as Hope, Joy, and Peace.

Caleb was diligent and bright. The food provided for the students was not like he had been accustomed to in the Madame's home, and soon he began losing weight. When the Madame came to see him, she asked Elisabeth, "What are you feeding these students?"

"Well, Madame, you know we can't afford to feed them like you eat. We try to feed them like the average Chinese eats in his own home. We believe they're as well or better fed than they'd be at home. We can't make exceptions."

"I know you like chicken," the Madame told Caleb. "I'll have the cook bring you a chicken once a week."

"Oh, no, Madame," Caleb exclaimed. "No meat is served in this hospital. I can eat like the others."

Somewhat taken aback, the Madame, nevertheless, did send him baskets of food from time to time—sweet cakes and fruit that he could share with the other students. Caleb became one of Elisabeth's prize students, and it was a happy day for her when he was baptized during the second year of his training.

As always, Elisabeth worked hard, going far beyond the call of duty. By the summer of her second year she felt she needed a vacation. Madame Chiang Kai-shek's sister, Madame Kung, invited Elisabeth to go with her family to Kuling, the summer resort in the mountains.

"Thank you very much," Elisabeth told Madame Kung. "I do need a vacation, and I've never been to Kuling."

Not too many days before Elisabeth was to join Madame Kung, Dr. Miller received an urgent telephone call. "It's Madame Chiang Kai-shek," the telephone operator told him. When Dr. Miller came back from the call, he said to Elisabeth, "You can't guess what that call was about. Madame Chiang Kai-shek wants to know if you won't come and join her and the General for your vacation instead of going with her sister to Kuling."

"Well, where is she, and how long does she want me to stay?

I've had my heart set on going to Kuling."

"She and the General and a considerable staff are in Chengtu, in far-away Szechwan Province, almost on the border of Tibet. The Generalissimo wants to visit some of these far-away provinces and learn first-hand what the conditions are in the country. He gets so many conflicting reports that he wants to know the truth for himself. That's why they've gone up there." The doctor paused and then continued. "But it seems they couldn't find a very good place to live in Chengtu, and all of them are getting sick. The Madame wants you to come and find out why they're all in such poor health. What about it, will you go?"

"What do you say? Do you think I should?"

"It will be for only a few weeks during the summer," he said. "And I think, Miss Redelstein, that you should."

"How will I go?"

"The Madame says that Mr. Donald will be flying up from Hankow, and you can go with him."

In Hankow Elisabeth stayed at the mission compound. And she contacted Mr. Donald, who was one of the Generalissimo's most dependable advisers. "We'll have to wait until the weather clears up," Donald told her. "We need good weather when we fly over the mountains beyond Ichang. The way it's pouring rain now, I don't know when we'll take off. I'll keep in touch with the airport and let you know just as soon as the 'all clear' is given."

It rained and it rained and it rained!

The Madame wired Donald, "Why aren't you here yet? We're waiting for you."

Donald told Elisabeth about the wire. "But we're not going to risk our necks just because they're in a hurry," he said. "We'll go when we're sure we can make it."

Finally they took off. But after flying for about two hours, they hit a low ceiling of black clouds. The clouds obliterated the mountains. "It's impossible to think of flying over the mountains in conditions like this," Donald sputtered. "Turn around and fly back to Hankow," he told the pilot.

After another week of waiting, the call came, "Can you be ready in fifteen minutes? We have a good weather report." Elisabeth was ready when the car came for her.

At the airport they found that the torrential rains had made a mess of the field. The airport commander told Elisabeth and Mr. Donald, "If you're going with that German pilot, tell him to take only half a load or he'll never get off the ground." When they entered the plane, they were surprised to see it filled with Chinese military men. Evidently these soldiers had also been waiting to get to Chengtu.

Donald stood at the front of the cabin, his cap at a rakish angle, looking every bit the casual Australian that he was. "Sorry, gentlemen, the airport commander says we'll never get off this muddy airfield if we try to fly with a full load." He paused. "If some of you have business that is not too important, perhaps you can get off and wait for the next plane."

Not a man moved, not an eyelid flickered. A man would lose face to admit that his work was not as important as another's. Elisabeth fidgeted in her seat. Donald stood watching them, the twinkle in his blue eyes changed to glinting steel. "Well," he said, "I see you men all have important business, so I will get off."

Elisabeth jumped to her feet. "If you are getting off, I am getting off too."

"No, you stay here. The Madame is waiting for you in Chengtu." Without another glance at the military, he picked up his bag and left. Several minutes ticked by and then one by one several of the military officers got off.

Half an hour later, Donald came back and got on the plane again. "You see now why I told you to stay," he whispered. "I knew I'd be back. I just had to get the ball rolling."

After a beautiful flight over the famous Yangtze River gorges, they landed in Chengtu.

"This was the only house we could find in the whole city,"

the Madame told Elisabeth when she arrived. Looking at the big ugly house, Elisabeth wondered how the Madame liked living in a place like that.

"I want you to make a survey of this whole place," the Madame said. "Something must be wrong, but I can't look after the servants' quarters and everything else with all I have to attend to. We've all had dysentery and fever. I'll appreciate anything you can do to find the trouble and make improvements."

The next day Elisabeth began her survey. Methodically, she inspected the house, the separate kitchen, the storehouse, the laundry, and the servants' quarters. In every place she listed the conditions she found and her suggested improvements.

The kitchen was the main trouble source. The tile roof of the small building radiated the sun's heat, making the building with its mud floor and unfinished walls, too hot. Cobwebs hung like dirty lace mantillas from rafters and corners. Flies as thick as raisins in a pie walked over the food. "We've got to get rid of these flies the first thing," Elisabeth decided. "And all the food has to be covered."

"I want to go to town with you," she told the majordomo (the one in charge of all the servants).

"Oh, Madame, this is no town for a foreign lady to be walking on the streets. What do you want? I'll get it for you."

"I have to see what's available before I know what I want," she explained. She knew that he didn't want to be seen on the street with a foreign she-devil!

Much against his wishes, she went to town with him. After looking around the market stalls at the tinsmith's and the wiresmith's goods, she decided that sieves were the best solution to the fly problem. She bought sieves of all sizes and shapes.

When she got back to the kitchen, she told the servants, "Any time food is out of that cupboard, it's to be covered with one of these sieves. If you're working on the food, all right, but when you're through, cover it with a sieve." She also brought mosquito netting and had a "screened" door made, but the servants left the door standing open most of the time.

"If that thing is an ice box," Elisabeth scoffed as she looked at the strange little box in one corner of the kitchen, "then it must have come out of Noah's ark." Only ten pounds of ice could be put in the top compartment, and under that a small door opened into a cubicle where food was kept.

Elisabeth opened the door, then drew back. Everything was slimy. And the odors! Nothing was covered. The strong-smelling Chinese foods were blending their odors with the Madame's coffee cream and other foreign foods.

"Everything in this box has to be covered," she told the servants. "Tomorrow morning we'll clean out that ice box." The next morning when she went to the kitchen, she said, "Now we'll clean the ice box."

"Oh, Madame," the majordomo said smugly, "we've already cleaned it."

But when Elisabeth looked in, she saw no change. "No," she said, "I mean really clean it. Get a pan of hot water and put some soda in it. Take everything out. Now wash the inside thoroughly and dry it."

The servants complied, but Elisabeth could tell by their facial expressions that they were thinking, "Crazy foreigners! *Hot* water! Doesn't she know we have to carry the water and then build a fire to heat it!"

"When you've finished the survey," the Madame told Elisabeth, "we'll call the servants and go over things with them." When Elisabeth was ready, the servants lined up and the two women stood facing them. "Now," the Madame said, "Miss Redelstein is here to attend to some things that I can't take care of because I'm too busy. I expect full cooperation from every one of you. If anyone feels that it's too hard to work with her, you just hunt for another job."

Soon Elisabeth had the cooperation of all the servants except the cook. In China the kitchen is the cook's domain, and he doesn't want any foreign she-devil messing around his kitchen.

The Madame asked Elisabeth to prepare the menu for each

day and give it to the cook. "We're going to live simply like the Americans do," she explained. "The Generalissimo says we can't expect the people to practice economy and simplicity unless we set the example. Even when we're having high-ranking officials to dinner, I want the meal to be simple."

Accordingly, Elisabeth each day made out the menu for the next day's dinner. But the cook could not understand. He'd say, "Do you know who is coming for dinner tomorrow?"

"Yes, I know."

"And you'd serve him a meal like that, with only *one* meat course! It's an insult." And so the cook would squeeze in an extra course of chicken or fish.

The cook also couldn't see the importance of keeping food covered in the ice box. More than once Elisabeth found food there without a cover.

One morning while the maid combed the Madame's hair, Elisabeth sat chatting with her. "How are things going in the kitchen?" the Madame asked. "Are you getting cooperation from the servants?"

"Yes. Except for the cook."

"What about the cook?"

"He can't see the importance of keeping food covered in the ice box."

Later that afternoon Elisabeth was surprised to learn that the Madame had gone to the kitchen, looked in the ice box, and had seen a pitcher of canned pears there without a cover. "Why are these pears not covered?" she demanded. While the cook stammered for an answer, she took the pitcher of pears to the middle of the room and dumped the whole thing on the floor. "I told you," she said, "that if you couldn't work with Miss Redelstein you could look for another job. This would be a good time to do it." Soon a more cooperative cook was on the job.

The flies and uncovered food were not the only problems in the kitchen. Elisabeth discovered that 20 bodyguards, who lived nearby, were coming into the kitchen every morning, each man carrying his own wash basin and towel. They helped themselves to hot water, lining up at the wash stand to wash their faces and brush their teeth.

"That doesn't seem very sanitary to me," Elisabeth told the Madame.

"I didn't know anything about this," the Madame said.

Elisabeth ordered improvements made in the quarters where the bodyguards lived. She also improved the servants' quarters, and arranged for hot water in one of the buildings, so they wouldn't have to come to the kitchen for it.

A tall German military officer, Captain Stennes, commanded the bodyguards. Sometimes he seemed to have as much trouble with them as Elisabeth had with the servants. Mr. Donald also spent the summer with them at Chengtu, frequently flying back to Hankow or Nanking or Shanghai on business for the Generalissimo. Stennes and Donald did not live at the Generalissimo's, but had their own accommodations in the city.

Gradually Elisabeth accomplished many changes, and the staff's health improved. However, Madame herself suffered severe anemia and needed a transfusion. The call went out for blood donors, but Chinese are hesitant about donating their own blood. Finally a Scottish professor at the University of Chengtu offered blood. His matched the Madame's, and so she had the transfusion and began to improve.

Life was simple and pleasant in Chengtu. Every day between tea and dinner, the Madame, the General, Captain Stennes, Mr. Donald when he was there, and Elisabeth went for a walk on the city wall. From the wall they could look out over the valley and watch the contests of flying kites. Kite flying was a great pastime in Chengtu, not only for children, but also for grown-ups, the city fathers, and even the military. Kites of all shapes, sizes, and colors sailed in the sky, even singing kites with varying tones.

Chengtu lies in a valley which grows scorching hot in the summertime. "I've got to get out of this heat," the Madame told the Generalissimo. "Can't we go up to Mount Omei for a few weeks?"

"There's no reason why you and Miss Redelstein can't go. Take as much of the staff as you need," the Generalissimo said. "I'll go with you, but I'll have to come back to the officers' training camp. I'll spend as much time as I can with you."

After several delays, the party packed up and headed for the mountain. When Elisabeth boarded the ferry boat to cross the river, she found that they were being wound across the river by a pully wheel. Once on the other side, she found out that she would be carried in a sort of native hammock. Sedan chairs were provided for the Madame and the Generalissimo, but the captain of the security guard had arranged for hammocks for Elisabeth and the maid.

Once aloft on the shoulders of four men, Elisabeth tried to relax and enjoy the new experience. But her stomach didn't take to the gentle bouncing. "Before I heave, I'd better give up and get out of here," she said to herself. Calling to the coolies to stop, she told them she would walk the rest of the way. The mountain is about 12,000 feet high, and they were going up 5,000 feet.

They finally reached their living quarters. A group of cottages belonging to missionaries who were not using them at present became their "home." These cottages were put together entirely by wooden pegs, because that part of the country has very little metal. The cottage in which the Generalissimo, the Madame, and Elisabeth lived had a small upstairs room which became Elisabeth's room. It was only a small cottage, but there was one bedroom for the Generalissimo and the Madame. There was no living room, but a screened-in porch served the purpose nicely. One little corner became the Generalissimo's study. Another tiny room was the "bathroom." There was no running water. A flat piece of tin with a six-inch rim around it constituted the bathtub. The "bathroom" did not boast a flush toilet, but had a one-holer chair with a pail underneath. Coolies emptied the pail every morning. The day after their arrival the Madame looked around and said, "This place is small, but it is all right. The only thing I don't like about it is that everyone can hear everyone else change his mind."

"Since water is so scarce, and the amount allotted each person for a bath is so small," Elisabeth suggested to the Madame, "why don't we share the bath water? I'm not afraid to bathe after you. I know you're very clean."

"All right," the Madame said. "If it's agreeable with you, it certainly is with me. It will be nice not to feel like I'm bathing in a teacup."

The Madame still did not feel well. One day she said to Elisabeth, "I know why I'm not feeling as well as I should. I haven't been studying the Bible enough. Let's have more Bible study." From then on she and Elisabeth studied the Bible together every day. The Madame kept a notebook with her, and when she came across some passage that especially appealed to her, she would say, "That is something that will help the Generalissimo," and she would make a note of it. Then she used those passages in her devotions with him. The Generalissimo and the Madame had devotions together every morning, no matter how early he had to go away on business.

The Generalissimo apparently did not realize how thin the ceiling-partition was between his study and Elisabeth's upstairs bedroom. Many times at night she heard him praying aloud. He pleaded with the Lord for wisdom to know how to work for his country and his people. Elisabeth lay in bed listening to those earnest prayers, almost scared to move lest the bed squeak and he realize that she could hear.

Although there was no running water, a very small power unit provided the cottage with electricity. The electricity was turned off after bedtime. Everybody carried a flashlight—everybody except Elisabeth, that is.

"You really ought to have a flashlight," Captain Stennes told her. After a few nights she decided he was right, for sleeping with rats running all over her was an experience she didn't enjoy. The flashlight sent them scampering away, and left her free to sleep.

The Generalissimo spent most of his time at the military training camp in the valley, but he came up for weekends and whenever else he could.

One day word came that there were thirty cases of groceries waiting at the foot of the mountain for the Madame and Elisabeth. "I didn't order those things, and I don't want them brought up here when we don't know how long we'll be here," Elisabeth declared. "I'll go down and check to see what they are." So a day was set when she would go down the mountain. But it rained so hard during the night that the roads were almost impassable.

"I thought you were going down to the valley today," Mr. Donald said the next morning.

"Look how it's rained," she said. "I can't go on a day like this."

"Sure you can go if you really want to," Mr. Donald chuckled. "You can borrow the captain's shorts, and I'll lend you my boots."

"That's what you think," Elisabeth replied.

Later in the day, the Madame said something about this being the day she had planned to go to the valley. "I told her she could go if she wanted to," Donald grinned. "She could borrow the captain's shorts and my boots."

The Madame laughed gleefully. "She couldn't get into the captain's shorts."

"Oh, I wouldn't be so sure about that," Elisabeth countered, thinking of the tall thin captain.

"I'm sure you can't," the Madame challenged.

"What makes you think so?"

"They'd be too tight. You couldn't squeeze into them."

"OK. You get the shorts, and I'll show you."

"You have to be able to sit down in them."

Years later at a party in Taiwan, the Madame said, "Miss Redelstein is the only one who ever outguessed me." The two of them enjoyed a good laugh over that experience.

7
Nanking

After three weeks on Mount Omei, the Madame announced that they would be going to Nanking for a few days. "The Generalissimo has a very important meeting there," she told Elisabeth. "We won't be gone long, so don't take much with you."

"Well, you have things everywhere, but I don't," Elisabeth said. "I think I'd better take a little more."

At three o'clock that afternoon, the Generalissimo came up the mountain from Chengtu. "Oh, just to get away from that heat for a little while," he said, taking a deep breath of the fresh mountain air. "Let me relax here for a few hours, and then we'll go down the hill this evening when it's cooler."

A few hours later they walked down the mountain. At the foot, waiting cars whisked them away to their house in Chengtu where they spent the night.

Elisabeth looked over the wardrobe she had brought from Shanghai. "The Madame says we'll be gone for only a few days," she thought, "but one never knows." She remembered the Sister in the convent telling her never to leave a room in a condition that she wouldn't want someone else to find it if she never got back. She double-checked her bureau drawers to make sure everything was in order. Then she packed. The next day they flew to Nanking.

Life in Nanking was different from anything Elisabeth had known before. The Generalissimo and the Madame lived in a large comfortable house on the grounds of the military academy. The furnishings reflected the Generalissimo's insistence on plain living when in Nanking, but the Madame had brought enough art treasures from her home in Shanghai to add touches of beauty here and there. Elisabeth and the Madame appreciated the modern conveniences after Omei, especially the bathroom.

As general supervisor of the household, Elisabeth helped plan dinners for foreign diplomats and officers. She also saw that the table was properly set with the good China and linens. A party of fifty guests always exhausted their supply of dishes, and she would have to borrow dishes. After this had happened two or three times, Elisabeth said to the Madame, "I think we ought to have enough dishes to serve an official dinner party without having to borrow."

"I think so too. You make out a list of what is needed."

Elisabeth figured out how many place settings of their pattern would be needed and the cost and gave the list to the Madame. "Isn't that a lot of money?" the Madame asked.

"Since when did you start worrying about the price of anything you want?" Elisabeth asked in surprise.

"Well, what do you expect of me after putting Scottish blood in my veins?" the Madame countered.

In the afternoons when the Generalissimo and the Madame lay down for a siesta, Elisabeth walked through the city or enjoyed the park. The first day when she left the house, the sentry at the gate did not question her. But by the time she returned, the sentry had been changed, and the new soldier challenged her: "Where are you going?"

"I am going to the Generalissimo's house."

"Ha, ha, ha, the Generalissimo's house! What are you going to do there?"

"I live there."

"Ha, ha, ha. You live there! Who ever heard of such a thing, a foreigner living in the Generalissimo's house! Ha, ha, ha."

"Here is my official pass." Elisabeth took from her purse the pass the Generalissimo had given her and showed it to the guard.

"*Ai yeh*! My mistake. So sorry." With much bowing the guard swung the gate wide for her to enter. The next day the same thing happened again and for three or four days until the word got around that a foreigner was living in the Generalissimo's house.

The Generalissimo had arranged with the German government to send a contingent of military experts as army advisers. Forty-six of them—with their families—came and established their headquarters at Nanking. They lived in a colony by themselves in attractive modern homes, not far from the military academy.

Soon after Elisabeth's arrival in Nanking, the Madame said, "I want you to meet His Excellency General Alexander von Falkenhausen, the head of the German advisory group."

"It will be good to meet another German. I hope he is as nice as Captain Stennes."

"Oh, he is."

The next time the German general called, the Madame arranged to have Elisabeth meet him. "He looks more like a lawyer or a doctor than a soldier," Elisabeth thought as she greeted the man standing stiffly straight in military fashion.

The general proved to be gracious and charming. "Ah," he said with a smile "maybe Fräulein Redelstein can interpret for us. Yes, Madame? You know my English is not good."

"That is a good idea, general," the Madame agreed. Elisabeth had a hunch that that was what the Madame had in mind all the time. From that time on, whenever the advisers had a problem to discuss with the Generalissimo, they came to Elisabeth and explained it to her in German. She translated it into English for the Madame, who in turn translated the message to the Generalissimo in Chinese. When he had reached a decision on the matter, he would tell the Madame. She would repeat it to Elisabeth in English. "Now," she would say, "you make an appointment with General von Falkenhausen and tell him what we have decided."

When Mussolini discovered that Chiang Kai-shek had military

advisers from Germany working for him, he asked to send aviators to operate the Generalissimo's planes and to advise him on developing an air force. These Italian advisers also lived with their families in Nanking. When they learned that Elisabeth spoke French, they asked her to interpret for them because their English was even poorer than that of the Germans. And so Elisabeth found herself in the role of an international interpreter.

The few days that the Generalissimo had said they would be in Nanking lengthened into weeks. Since it appeared that they were not going back to Chengtu, Captain Stennes was sent there to bring the things that had been left. When he returned he said to Elisabeth, "It was a pleasure to find your things in such neat order. It was no trouble at all to pack them."

"The result of my convent training," she said.

During the remaining summer weeks in Nanking the Generalissimo and the Madame often took little excursions. Sometimes they went to a lake, sometimes to the mountains. They liked picnicking in nature. Elisabeth accompanied them on these excursions. It fell to her to plan the lunch and arrange for its being served. At first they had only boxes in which to carry the food and equipment. "I wish we had something more convenient than these boxes," Elisabeth said one day.

"Why don't you see if you can't find something in the stores?" the Madame suggested. The next time Elisabeth went to Shanghai she looked in the large Wing-On department store. There she found a German-made basket equipped with plastic dishes and eating utensils. It was a small matter to add chop sticks. The next time they went on a picnic, the Madame asked the Generalissimo, "What do you think of this arrangement for carrying our things?"

"It is very nice. Is it the product of our country?"

Knowing how anxious the Generalissimo was to promote the use of all national products and only national products, avoiding the use of foreign things as much as possible, Elisabeth hesitated. "I bought it in Wing-On's," she said, hoping that would satisfy him. It did.

The Generalissimo loved to go back to his home province, where he had already established a provincial government free from graft and where living conditions among the average citizens had been greatly improved. Sometimes they flew there for a weekend.

Often at night Elisabeth slipped back into the role of nurse and gave the Madame a good massage. "I always sleep like a baby after your massages," the Madame would say. Without the back rubs she seemed restless and nervous, unable to sleep.

Eventually the Generalissimo decided that he must return to Chengtu to see how things were going at the military training camp. He wanted the Madame to go along, but she didn't want to. She told Elisabeth, "In the morning I want you to go to the airport early and tell the captain of the security that he can rearrange the seating, because you and I and my maid will not be going. I don't want my husband to know, lest he insist I go, and I wouldn't want to hold out against him."

Early the next morning Elisabeth went to the airport and gave Captain Stennes the message. She was still there when the Generalissimo and the Madame arrived. Not until the last minute did the Madame tell her husband that she was not going. "I have some important business to attend to in Shanghai," she told him.

"You be sure to come later then. I'll be waiting for you," he said in farewell.

"Now we can go to Shanghai," the Madame told Elisabeth. She seemed pleased that she had sent the Generalissimo off alone without an argument. In Shanghai they lived in the Madame's home in the French Concession. Mr. Donald was also in Shanghai at the time and more or less took orders from the Madame.

The Generalissimo kept wiring for the Madame to come to Chengtu. He even sent a big plane to bring her, but she had no intention of going. "That plane can just stay here so all the army officers can't fly around in it as they usually do," she said.

Also during this time, in a gesture of friendship, Mussolini gave a luxury plane to the Generalissimo. The plane had the latest and best of everything, even to a bar. "We don't need a bar," the Madame declared. "We ought to have the interior remodeled. See that the bar is taken out and the interior is remodeled. Put in a cot or something where we can stretch out. Make an appointment with an interior decorator and have the changes made."

Elisabeth contacted an interior decorator and met him at the airport at eight o'clock in the morning. She had also phoned the Italian pilots of the plane and asked them to meet her at the airport at eight o'clock. The next morning she and the decorator were there, but no pilots. Fortunately, someone else at the airfield had a key to the plane. She explained to the decorator just what they wanted to have done. As they were leaving the airport, here came the Italian pilots. They seemed much surprised that she had already been on the plane.

"Your appointment was for eight o'clock," she told them, trying to sound authoritative like the Madame. "All arrangements have been made. We don't need you anymore today."

The pilots looked a bit sheepish and annoyed. Elisabeth knew how they felt. The Italians always resented doing things at the direction of the Madame. They called China the petticoat government, because the Madame was the one they had to deal with. Of course, it was only natural since she knew English and the Generalissimo did not.

Mr. Donald decided to go back to Nanking and took passage on a boat to sail at midnight. Elisabeth sat alone reading that evening, waiting for the Madame to return from visiting her sister. When the Generalissimo was away, she slept in the same room with the Madame. After ten o'clock the telephone rang. "Miss Redelstein!" The Madame's voice sounded urgent, "I need Mr. Donald tomorrow morning. Please get him off that boat." Elisabeth promptly called a car and went to the boat to get Mr. Donald off before it sailed.

Donald laughed as they walked off the boat together. "The folk on the boat will say, 'Uh huh, the old man thought he was getting away, but the old lady came after him and pulled him off the boat.' "

"The Madame said for me to put you up at the Grand Hotel," Elisabeth told Donald. "She will get in touch with you in the morning." At the hotel, she applied for a room for Mr. Donald. The clerk showed them three or four rooms but all with two beds in them. "He only needs a single room," Elisabeth explained, but they didn't seem to have any. Elisabeth and Donald decided he could occupy a double room for one night. In the morning the Madame phoned him, and he stayed on in Shanghai to help her look after some important matters.

Within a few weeks the Madame and Elisabeth returned to Nanking, and the Generalissimo came back shortly thereafter. While in Nanking Elisabeth went to church each Sabbath and became well acquainted with the missionaries and the national believers there. They were in the midst of building a new chapel. Unfortunately, the building contractor absconded with a considerable amount of their money before the building was finished. The church appealed to the mission for funds to complete the building, but no funds were available. The local believers were doing everything they could to raise money to finish their chapel.

When Elisabeth joined the Madame, nothing had been said about her wages. As it turned out, the Madame paid her exactly double what she had been receiving at the sanitarium. She sent her regular tithes and offerings to the office in Shanghai, based on the salary they had paid her. Then she gave the difference between that figure and what the Madame paid her to the local church to apply on the new chapel.

Elisabeth enjoyed life with the Generalissimo and the Madame and with the fellow believers. The German advisers and their families became her friends, entertaining her often in their homes. But this could not go on forever. It had now been nine months since she left the Shanghai Sanitarium, and so she was not surprised to receive Dr. Miller's message, "You are urgently needed at the training school. Please come back as soon as the Madame can release you."

"I hate like sin to see you go," the Madame said, "but my country's interests must come ahead of my personal interests, and I realize that you have all those young students there in the training school. You can tell them what the Generalissimo and I are aiming at, what we are trying to do. You can help secure their cooperation in making China a better place to live. For that reason, I'm willing to let you go."

As a parting gift, she gave Elisabeth a beautiful soapstone carving. It was an unusual piece, depicting an old wise man with three or four of the "spirits" serving him. In China the aged are honored for their wisdom.

When the servants learned that Elisabeth was leaving, they bought her another soapstone carving, a smaller one than the Madame's but also very beautiful. Elisabeth's heart was touched by the servants' gift. It showed that they appreciated what she had done to make their lives easier.

General von Falkenhausen gave Elisabeth a farewell party in his home and made a speech saying how much they would miss her. Little did she dream under what circumstances her path and the general's would cross again.

On the way to Shanghai she stopped off in Hankow to visit her good friends, Mr. and Mrs. E. C. Wood. Mr. Wood, the division builder, was now engaged in building the Wuhan Sanitarium outside Hankow. While there she received another wire from Dr. Miller: "Would you be willing to accompany prominent Chinese lady to Europe?"

8

With Madame Chang Hsueh-liang in England

Elisabeth did not answer the doctor's telegram. It seemed too preposterous a suggestion. As soon as she arrived in Shanghai and saw Dr. Miller, she asked, "What is the idea of sending me that telegram about going to Europe? First you wire that I'm urgently needed here; then before I get here you want to know if I'll go to Europe with a Chinese lady."

"Oh, Miss Redelstein," the doctor explained, "it is Madame Chang Hsueh-liang. She's homesick to see her children who are studying in England. She cannot go alone, because she doesn't understand the languages. The Marshal can't go with her, and he asked me if we had anyone who could accompany his wife for two months. We thought of you because you know the languages. How do you feel about it?"

"To be perfectly frank with you, Doctor, I'm not interested. I had to leave Madame Chiang Kai-shek where I was enjoying life, and I'm eager to get back to work at the training school. To go with this woman I don't even know—well, I'm not much interested."

"You think about it a few days and then give me your answer," the doctor said.

"I know he expects me to go," Elisabeth thought. "And in the end he'll probably get his way." Her jaw set in a firm line as she watched the doctor walk away.

While Elisabeth was still considering the request, Madame Chiang Kai-shek came to Shanghai. She telephoned Elisabeth and asked if they could go for a ride together. As the chauffeur headed toward Woosong, the Madame in her more-Western-than-Chinese way came directly to the point. "I wanted to talk with you about this proposed trip with Madame Chang Hsueh-liang. This poor soul is dying to see those children, and she cannot go alone. It would be real missionary work if you would go with her. Of course–" the Madame grinned– "after living with me you will find it kind of dullish living with her. You'll have to take the initiative in everything. But I wish you would go. It would really be missionary work."

"Well, all right. If you feel that way, I'll do it," Elisabeth agreed unenthusiastically. "I'll have to turn the training school over to someone else again, but since it is to be for only two months, I guess they can get along without me–even if Dr. Miller did say I was urgently needed!"

When Mr. Donald heard about the trip, he offered some advice. "Be sure she understands that you are not going as her personal maid," he said. "Let her know that you'll take charge of the trip, but that you are not going to pack her bags and do all the things she is accustomed to having servants do for her. Be sure she takes her personal maid along."

"Thank you for that advice," Elisabeth said. "I certainly have no intention of being anyone's personal maid." She told Dr. Miller she would go on one condition–that she be allowed to visit her parents while in Europe.

Toward the end of April, 1936, the party set sail on an Italian vessel–the Madame, her sister-in-law (the younger sister of Chang Hsueh-liang), the maid, and Elisabeth. The trip called for stopovers in Hong Kong, Singapore, and Djibuti.

In Venice, Elisabeth and her party were taken by gondola to catch the train for Paris, where they were to visit the brother of Chang Hsueh-liang. They went first to the brother-in-law's home. Later Elisabeth was taken to the Hotel St. John where she stayed while they were in Paris.

"You must stay awhile and see the sights of Paris," the Madame's brother-in-law urged.

"No, I want to get on to London and see my children,"

Madame Chang Hsueh-liang said. "Can't you get a reservation for us tomorrow?"

"You can't get a reservation for four people on such short notice as that!"

Turning to Elisabeth, the Madame pleaded, "You do something."

Next morning Elisabeth went to Cooks Travel Agency and asked them for the earliest reservation possible for a party of four traveling on Chinese diplomatic passports. With no little effort on their part, the agents at Cooks secured reservations for three o'clock that same afternoon.

Thanking them, Elisabeth hurried out to get a taxi. She gave the brother-in-law's address to the driver, but he said he'd never heard of such an address. Perplexed, she rushed back into Cooks to see if someone there could give the driver directions. But no one there was familiar with that address either.

"Take me to the Hotel St. John," she told the driver. She knew she could find her way from the hotel to the Chinese gentleman's home. The driver stopped before a building bearing the name "Hotel St. John." "That's not the hotel where I stayed last night." Elisabeth was now fully exasperated.

"Well, you can see it says Hotel St. John," the driver countered.

"Take me to the Chinese Embassy," she directed, and gave him the address. At the embassy she appealed for someone to tell the driver how to get to the home of the brother of Chang Hsueh-liang. In no time they were there. The driver had taken her to the Hotel St. John in the city rather than to the one in Neuilly where the Marshal's brother lived.

Elisabeth ran up the steps and persistently rang the bell. "We have reservations for three o'clock this afternoon." The words spilled out as soon as she saw the Madame. "There's no time to lose if we're going to make the plane."

"Oh, we can't go until after lunch."

"There's no time to eat."

"You have to stay and eat. We cooked carrots especially for

you, so you would have some vegetable."

Elisabeth's heart dropped. What else could she do but try to be polite and eat her carrots since they'd been cooked especially for her. Then she took a taxi to the hotel to get her baggage, while the Madame, her sister-in-law, and the maid went in the brother-in-law's car to the airport. Before boarding the plane, Elisabeth wired their arrival time to the embassy in London and to the children. It fell to Elisabeth, too, to fill out all the forms required of anyone going to England–Why are you going there? What are you going to do there? How long are you going to stay? and so on. Once aboard the plane all went well as they flew over the Channel, but as the plane started coming down for a landing, Elisabeth's carrots came up!

Off the plane, Elisabeth told the other ladies, "You wait for me at the customs station while I take care of the passports," which had to be checked and stamped. Then she joined them at the customs check point. The official asked, "Anything to declare?"

"No," Elisabeth assured him. "Only yesterday we arrived in Paris. We have had no time to go shopping."

"Would you mind opening that box, please?" She opened the box, and there, staring back at her in all their finery, three new spring bonnets with the price tags still on them. Embarrassed, Elisabeth tried to explain. "I was busy all morning getting reservations. I did not know that the Madame and her sister had gone shopping." At that point the official saw the passports in her hand. "Oh, Madam, I see you have diplomatic passports. I apologize. Go right through. No questions."

The Madame's three children (Pauline, 21; Martin, 20; and Raymond, 18) waited on the other side of the fence. The family reunion was warm and eager. The young people had already rented a car and a villa in Brighton Hove on the seashore. The only thing left to do was to move in.

But it wasn't quite that simple. There must be servants to do the work of the household. At the employment agency Elisabeth hired a cook, a maid, and a chauffeur. Although she had servants in Germany and in China, this was something different–hiring and working with servants in England.

What with England's cool May weather and a house without central heating, Elisabeth and her Chinese party found the place to be very chilly. They heaped on blankets and cuddled hot water bottles between their feet at night, and they shivered through the day. The fireplace created a cozy atmosphere in its immediate vicinity, but failed to penetrate the chill ten feet away. Doorway draperies separated the living room from the dining room.

"Let's pull back the draperies in the morning and have a fire in the fireplace in each room," Elisabeth said to the cook, thinking thereby to diffuse the heat over a wider area.

"Not in both places at the same time!" the cook exclaimed.

"Yes," Elisabeth insisted, "in both places at the same time!"

"Whoever heard of the like–in both places at the same time! You can only be in one place at one time."

"Listen," Elisabeth said, slightly exasperated, "am I paying for the coal, or am I not? If I am paying for the coal, why can't we have a fire where we want it?" After that they had a fire in both fireplaces, and Elisabeth rented a gas heater for the little den off the living room. At last they were comfortable.

Pauline, who had been in boarding school, moved in with her mother and her aunt. The boys roomed and boarded in the home of one of the professors, but every afternoon they came for tea and stayed for dinner. Elisabeth planned meals around the program of the family. Believing the British custom of a heavy dinner at night to be unhealthful, she planned their main meal at noon, a fairly ample teatime snack, and a light supper. Cooking in England differed from cooking in Germany or America. Vegetables were boiled in plain water and then lifted out onto the dinner plate. Each person could season them to suit himself from the three or four bottles of sauces on the table.

Once the family was settled and the servants knew what was expected of them, things ran smoothly.

Brighton Hove was a delightful place to live, especially as summer came on and the weather warmed up. Every afternoon Elisabeth and the others would walk along the seashore or drive far back into England's beautiful countryside.

Just as Madame Chiang Kai-shek had said, Elisabeth found life with Madame Chang Hsueh-liang very different from that in the Generalissimo's household. Madame Chiang Kai-shek was very Western in her thinking and actions, efficient and keenly interested in governmental affairs. Madame Chang Hsueh-liang was the typical well-bred Chinese lady, small and dainty, retiring in personality, but with a mind of her own and a will not easily crossed. "I can hardly say it is 'dullish,' however," Elisabeth thought. "For I never know what's going to happen next."

The Madame wanted to go shopping in London. Not being familiar with the stores herself, Elisabeth went to Cooks and asked for a list of the stores. The always helpful clerks at Cooks gave her a listing of the different shops, indicating which were the most exclusive shops that catered to the best people in London, and another list of less expensive but good shops. Elisabeth asked the Madame which shops she would prefer to visit.

"Oh, the most exclusive, of course," she said. She wanted to buy some gifts to take home to China, and decided upon the dresser sets for which England was rather famous—mirror, comb, brush, powder box, et cetera, enameled in silver or gold, and put up in silk-lined boxes.

In one of London's most exclusive shops, where she was waited upon by two tall Englishmen wearing black bow ties and cut-away coats, the Madame found just what she wanted, and she selected six sets. But she wanted them to be in different boxes, either arranged differently or with different colored silk linings.

Although the Madame did not understand or speak English well enough to travel abroad alone, she had picked up a smattering of phrases in China, and during the boat trip

Elisabeth had taught her a few important words and sentences. Now Elisabeth gasped as she heard the Madame say to the dignified clerks, "I buy many, you make little more cheap?" giving the full Chinese rising inflection to *cheap*.

One astonished salesman blinked his eyes and turned to Elisabeth, "What did the Madame say?"

Before Elisabeth could answer with an apology, the Madame repeated it, "I buy many, you make little more *cheap*?" Elisabeth had not told her that in London all shops are "one-price shops," and that there is no bargaining of price as is the custom in China.

The two dignified Englishmen put their heads together for a moment and then told the Madame that they would knock off a pound on each set. Elisabeth stood blushing with embarrassment while the boxes were being changed. But her blushes turned to swallowed laughter when the Madame got the bill—so much for the sets and so much for the boxes, which brought the total to exactly the same price they had quoted her in the beginning. The Madame went away happy, never realizing that there was no set price on the boxes and that the original price included the boxes.

Elisabeth rejoiced to find a Seventh-day Adventist church in Brighton Hove where she could attend services.

Writing to some of her friends in Shanghai about her experiences, she said, "The minister and all his members are so friendly they make me feel right at home. You know we sometimes think the Britishers in the Orient are a little uppish. That must be only the ones who go abroad, for I find the people here, especially in our church, to be very pleasant and hospitable. I doubly appreciate the Sabbath and the privilege of attending church with these dear people after having the family and the servants and the household problems to deal with every day during the week."

One day in June, Elisabeth approached the Madame. "I think it's time for me to go and visit my family in Germany," she said. "I'll be gone for a week or ten days, and when I come back and the boys and Pauline are out of school, we'll arrange to tour the continent."

In preparation for being gone, Elisabeth opened a checking account in the New York Bank of London so that the Madame could draw money as she needed it. But the Madame complained, "Oh, I am afraid I cannot cash a check, because I cannot write my name in English the same way every time. And if it is not the same, the bank may not accept the check, and I won't be able to get any money. I think I had better have the cash on hand and not have to bother with the bank."

Elisabeth and the children tried to tell her she should not have that much money in the house. But she insisted, and so again Elisabeth went to the bank, taking the Madame with her.

"I'm going away for a week or two," she told the clerk at the bank, "and the Madame is afraid she won't be able to write a check and sign it the same every time, and so she wants me to close out the account and give her the cash."

"You only opened the account a few days ago," the banker said in his clipped British speech. "We cannot understand your closing it out so soon."

Blushing, Elisabeth struggled for a reasonable-sounding answer. She knew that it looked suspicious for her to say she was going to Germany and at the same time ask to draw out the money. Again she explained the Madame's reason for wanting the money.

"If she could sign in Chinese, would that be all right?" the banker asked.

Elisabeth spoke to the Madame about it. "Oh, yes," she said. "I could sign checks in Chinese."

"Well, you have her sign the card now in Chinese, and we'll send a messenger with it to our branch bank in Brighton Hove this afternoon. Tomorrow you take her to the bank, have her sign a check in Chinese, and let her see that she can really cash the check."

The next day at the Brighton Hove branch, when the Madame saw that she could cash a check by signing her name in

Chinese, she was satisfied that she could get along while Elisabeth was gone.

Elisabeth breathed a little prayer as she set out for Germany, "Thank You, Lord, for helping to settle that matter; and may this be the last trouble I'll have with the family of Chang Hsueh-liang."

9

Trouble -- Physical and Political

The week with her family went all too quickly for Elisabeth. Trying to catch up with everything that had happened in their lives, sharing good food and old memories, as well as visiting familiar places made the hours rush away.

And soon Elisabeth returned to Brighton Hove. Early in July she and the family set out to spend the remainder of the summer traveling on the continent. First they would go to Paris to visit the children's uncle. From there they planned to visit Switzerland and Italy and return by way of Germany, getting back to London in time for the opening of the next school term.

They flew to Paris on a Sunday. When they arrived at their uncle's home, they learned that the Chinese embassy staff had arranged for a banquet on Monday night. All the Chinese officials in Paris came out to honor the wife and children of their highly respected field marshal, Chang Hsueh-liang. Elisabeth sat next to the younger son, Raymond, and watched the boy eat as course after course was brought on. It was as though he were starved for real Chinese food. Perhaps this was his first big banquet, and he was thoroughly enjoying it.

"Raymond," she whispered, "you are eating like a pig. Don't come to me if you have a stomachache." The boy laughed and went on eating.

Back at the hotel, the Madame seemed to be in a gayer mood than Elisabeth had ever seen her. The young people, too, were jolly in spite of their over-loaded stomachs, and all retired in a happy frame of mind.

The next morning, Martin came to Elisabeth, "Miss Redelstein, Raymond is feeling very bad. Won't you come and see if you can help?"

"Well, that's just what I expected after the way he ate last night," she said, heading for Raymond's room. Raymond was writhing in pain, perspiration dotting his forehead. Elisabeth called the American Hospital and asked for a doctor to come. From her description, the doctor suspected appendicitis, and so he brought a lab technician with him. Sure enough, by Tuesday afternoon the lab report confirmed that Raymond was suffering from appendicitis. Immediately they rushed him to the hospital for surgery.

The American who operated allowed Elisabeth to be in the operating room. When he opened the abdomen, he exclaimed, "Oh, there's a lot of free fluid here. Has this boy had typhoid?"

"I don't know," Elisabeth answered. "I haven't been with the family long enough to know much about their background."

The doctor sent a sample of the fluid to the lab, and it proved that at some time in his life Raymond had indeed had typhoid. After the surgery Elisabeth hired three nurses to special him around the clock in eight-hour shifts. For the first three days he did very well, but by the fourth day nothing had yet passed through his intestines since the operation, and the boy was feeling very bad indeed. Nearly a week passed with the same situation. By the following Monday Raymond's abdomen was so distended that the gas crowded against his heart causing erratic heart beat and shortness of breath.

"There's nothing else to do but to operate and relieve that pressure," the doctor decided after consultation. They asked the mother to sign the operating permit.

"No, I won't sign," she declared, half in tears. "If anything happens to Raymond, my husband will think it's my fault, and he'll put me away and take his concubine, Elsie Chow, as his number one wife. I'm not going to be responsible for that. You get permission from my husband if you want to operate. Send a cable to him."

Elisabeth, Pauline, and Martin exerted all their persuasive powers to convince her. They explained that by the time they sent a cable and got a reply, Raymond could be dead. Finally she signed the permit.

The operation revealed that the boy had developed a paralysis of the ileum. The doctors simply made an incision in the intestine to relieve the gas. They decided not to close the incision but to allow it to granulate—heal from the inside out—and so the hole in his side had to be dressed every day.

Raymond was still sick and required special nursing. Elisabeth hired an Australian nurse for the morning shift and an English nurse for the afternoon shift. But Raymond did not feel at ease with them. It was too difficult when he was so weak to try to talk to them in a foreign language. He liked Elisabeth because he could speak to her in Chinese. Every evening he would plead, "You won't leave me tonight, will you, Miss Redelstein?"

"No, Raymond, I'll be right here with you if you need anything," she'd reply. All night she sat in a chair by his bed, keeping her hand on him. As long as he felt her hand he would relax. As the boy grew weaker, Elisabeth called in three famous French doctors for consultation. They said there was nothing more that could be done. She tried to get a well-known German doctor that she knew about, but he was on vacation. Then she tried for another famous doctor in Germany, a Doctor Umber. He sent word that he would come as soon as he could. In the meantime, Raymond grew weaker and weaker. He could not eat, and lost a great deal of weight.

With every passing day the Madame became more excited. "If you could only get hold of Dr. Miller," she kept pleading with Elisabeth. "Send him a cable."

"I can't reach Dr. Miller," Elisabeth patiently repeated over and over. "He is on the high seas returning to China from America, and I don't know what ship he's on. There's no way I can get in touch with him."

The next day it was the same thing. "If you could only get in touch with Dr. Miller, he would have some method these doctors do not know about."

After hearing this for about the twentieth time, Elisabeth thought, "Maybe this is the reason God has put me here." Sometimes she had wondered why she should be traveling and looking after this family instead of training young people in Shanghai.

"Yes, Madame," she said, "Dr. Miller does have another method. But you are not a Christian, and you may not like his method. When Dr. Miller has done everything he can for a patient and things are not going well, he always says, 'We have done all we know how to do. Now it is time to call on the Great Physician to show His power.' Then we go into Dr. Miller's office and kneel down and pray to the great God in heaven. I know many, many people who have been healed in that way. But you are not a Christian, and unless you have faith to believe that God can heal your son, I'm not sure that He will do it."

"But can't you do something?" the Madame pleaded.

"Yes, I can send a cable and ask for prayer, and I can pray." Elisabeth cabled Shanghai: "Doctors despairing of Raymond's life. Request prayer."

In the middle of the night as Elisabeth sat by his bed, she realized that Raymond was very low. She thought he was dying and sent the nurse to bring the doctor. Again she felt his pulse and watched his respiration. They were quieting down and quieting down. "The end is near," she thought and prayed silently.

When the doctor and the nurse came in, the doctor looked at Raymond and said, "Oh, he's asleep. That's a good sign. Let him sleep as long as he will." Raymond slept for two and a half hours, the longest he'd slept at one time for several days.

The next day Dr. Umber from Germany arrived. "Miss Redelstein," he said as he looked at Raymond, "this is a different picture from what I expected."

"Yes, I think we passed the crisis in the night," she said.

Dr. Umber studied Raymond's records, made an outline for

Elisabeth to follow in his treatment, and asked her to keep in touch with him. Then he was on his way back to Germany. Elisabeth paid him $1,500 for his help.

From then on Raymond started improving and began taking liquids. He had been fed intravenously for many days. He needed a blood transfusion badly, but days went by and the lab did not come forth with blood.

"Why are you not giving this boy a blood transfusion?" Elisabeth asked.

"Sorry, but we have not been able to find a Chinese to give blood."

"Oh," Elisabeth exploded, "blood is the same the world over. You don't have to have Chinese blood!" Inside half an hour they arranged for a direct transfusion.

Every time Raymond ate or drank the dressing on his incision had to be changed because residue came out the hole. The first time he had noodle soup, Elisabeth fed him as usual, set the tray aside, and started to change the dressing. To her surprise, noodles kept coming out through the incision. Then she knew that the boy was not getting any nourishment at all. She reported it to the doctor.

He ordered X rays and found that by going into the abdomen when it was so distended, they had made the opening right next to the opening from the stomach into the intestines. And so when the stomach started working, it pushed the food out the incision instead of pushing it into the intestines.

The only solution seemed to be to plug the hole. Using sterilized cotton balls as plugs, they pulled the skin together in a fold over the opening and taped it down with adhesive. That worked, and soon Raymond began improving.

One day the Australian nurse said to Elisabeth, "You haven't been out of this hospital in six weeks. It's time you got out of here or you're going to crack up. Raymond is so much better that I want you to take the afternoon off. When the afternoon nurse comes on, you can go for an outing with me. I'll bring you back this evening."

Elisabeth marked Raymond's menu for the evening meal to make sure that everything would be all right. Then she went out and enjoyed a pleasant afternoon in the sunshine and fresh air.

When she returned in the evening, Raymond was in agony with acute indigestion. The nurse explained that Raymond had felt so much better and had been on a bland diet for so long that she wanted to do something nice for him. So she had asked the dietitian to fry some potatoes in butter for him. Raymond ate the potatoes and enjoyed them while they were going down, but now, oh, the terrible pain. Elisabeth called the doctor to give the boy a shot. From then on Raymond would not eat a bite unless Elisabeth authorized it.

By now Raymond looked like a skeleton. Elisabeth encouraged him to get lots of calories. "We will count your calories," she told him, "and when you get over a certain number a day your mother will reward you." The mother agreed with the idea.

Every day Raymond would ask, "If I eat this, how many calories will it be?" He had fun counting calories, and when he passed the goal his mother promised that as soon as he was out of the hospital she would buy him the air rifle he had been wanting. When he left the hospital eight weeks later, he had regained the thirty pounds he lost.

"Mother," Raymond said one day, "you don't know how close I have been to death's door. I would not be here today if the mission people had not prayed for me."

Now the mother wanted to know more about the God who was able to bring a person back from the very brink of the grave. Elisabeth got some books for her to read–very simple books about God and about Jesus. Every morning and evening the Madame would get on her knees to thank that God who had saved her son.

When the doctor first allowed Raymond to get up, Elisabeth put him into a wheelchair and wheeled him out into the hospital garden. When his mother found him out there, she was horrified. "Oh, why have you allowed him to get up," she cried, "when that little hole is still open?" That "little hole" was her constant worry. Of course clean dressings were kept on the opening, and it was slowly healing.

The family did not stay in the hotel all the time Elisabeth and Raymond were in the hospital. They took a nice apartment. When Raymond was finally released, he and Elisabeth moved into the apartment with them. Martin returned to school in England. The rest of the family stayed in Paris for another five weeks so that Raymond could see the doctor two or three times a week. Finally, the doctor released his patient and said it was safe for him to travel. The family then went to Nice on the French Riviera.

At the Riviera Elisabeth arranged for accommodations in one of the fine hotels. Since they had left their car in England, she rented a Rolls Royce to take them for drives. Their first ride provided a magnificent view of the Mediterranean as well as many villas of the wealthy who vacationed there. When it came time to pay the driver, the Madame complained, "That is too dear."

Most of the people who stayed at the hotel had their own cars and yachts. Elisabeth thought the Madame would want to live in the same style, but now she was complaining about the cost of hiring a car.

"All right," Elisabeth said, "we don't have to have a car. There are buses available here." Normally, only country people, servants, or limited-budget tourists rode the bus.

Three roads ran from Nice to Monaco, one along the seashore, one in the middle, and the most scenic, the high road, which wound around the mountain. Elisabeth arranged to go by bus on the high road and return by the seashore. The ancient vehicle coughed and sputtered its way along the high road. Before they were half way up the mountain the radiator began boiling and spewing steam.

"Let's get off this thing and take a taxi," the Madame more or less ordered.

"There's no way of getting a taxi here, half way up the

mountainside," Elisabeth replied calmly. After a couple of more kilometers the radiator boiled over again. While they all sat in the bus, waiting for it to cool off, the Madame looked around at the other passengers. Elisabeth sensed her inwardly shrinking from the others who were not of her class. After two or three more stops for the boiling radiator, they reached the top of the mountain. As soon as they stepped off the bus, the Madame announced, "We will take a taxi home."

"Oh, we're at the top now, going down won't be so bad," Elisabeth said. "Besides, how would we get a taxi to come away up here after us? We're going home by way of the seashore, the road is level there."

As the bus traveled down the mountain they glimpsed the Royal Palace on its 200-foot rock surrounded by beautiful gardens. They rolled on toward Monaco. Hotels and apartment buildings were scattered from the top of a high terraced bluff down to the edge of a natural harbor on the Mediterranean. In a charming little restaurant, where they could look out on the blue sea, they enjoyed dinner before boarding the bus again for the coastline ride back to their hotel.

That was the last bus ride! From then on a rented Rolls Royce convertible took them wherever the Madame wanted to go. Every afternoon at two o'clock the Rolls took them for a ride. Often they stopped at some interesting place along the way for tea and returned to the hotel for dinner. After a month of this relaxed living, Raymond gained another five pounds. The Madame, however, still worried about that "little hole."

The time had come to head back to England. Because of Raymond's illness and the consequent delay, he was already late for the opening of school. The two months that Elisabeth had agreed to travel with the Madame had turned into five.

"Whenever I commit myself to a time limit I seem to exceed it," she thought.

From the Riviera they went to Switzerland, and from Switzerland across Lake Constance to Friedrichshafen, where the zeppelin airships were built. The Madame decided that if they went to America they would go by zeppelin. At the airfield they saw one huge airship ready to take off for America. Elisabeth asked if they could go inside and see the cabin.

The doors had already been closed, but the officer allowed them to go inside. The Madame tried the beds and looked the cabin over to see if it was comfortable. Yes, she was sure that zeppelin was the way they would travel to America.

At Munich, Elisabeth's mother came from Ochsenhausen to spend a day with them.

After a short stopover in Cologne they flew back to England. It was November, and Elisabeth thought they would soon be going back to China, and so she got them all hotel rooms. However, within a few days the Madame decided she wanted to live in a house. So Elisabeth went house hunting. She found a house she liked, except that the bathroom resembled a bay window, with glass on three sides. "How do you heat this bathroom?" she asked the maid.

"Ma'm, we draw hot water when we take a bath in England."

Elisabeth thought she didn't want to depend on hot water as the only heat in the bathroom, so she didn't take that place. She found another house, however, that pleased everyone.

Then servants had to be hired again. Fortunately, Elisabeth was able to get the same chauffeur who had worked for them before. With a new cook and a new maid, they were all set to move into their new home.

After two weeks the chauffeur came to Elisabeth and said, "I'm embarrassed that one of my countrymen should be so ignorant, but the cook says she came to work on Sunday and you pay her on Tuesday, so you're cheating her out of two day's pay. Would you mind paying her on Sunday?"

Elisabeth and the Madame were making plans to return to China when the news came that Chang Hsüeh-liang had taken Chiang Kai-shek prisoner in North China. What a shock that news caused! The Chinese embassies from Paris and London phoned the Madame wanting to know what word she had received. She knew only what was in the newspapers. Then a cable came from Dr. Kung, finance minister in Nanking, asking the Madame to persuade her husband to release Chiang.

Throwing up her hands in desperation, she cried, "I can't advise my husband in a thing like that. I am not like Madame Chiang Kai-shek. My husband will not listen to me. I will not send any cable."

The Chinese students in London, a sizable group of them at that time, decided to demonstrate in front of the Madame's house and force her to do something. When Elisabeth learned of that, she let word get out that the Madame was leaving. She dismissed the cook and the maid, keeping only the chauffeur. Then the family lay low for several days until the excitement blew over.

A tense situation prevailed in China that winter of 1936-37, with the Japanese rattling their swords almost at the very gates of Peking, the spirit of nationalism growing stronger throughout the country, and the Communists exerting an ever expanding influence in North China. Chiang Kai-shek and Chang Hsueh-liang did not agree on which was the greater danger. Chang Hsueh-liang considered Japan the greater threat, since he had been driven out of Manchuria by the Japanese.

The Generalissimo, however, feared the Communists more, and so he sent the Young Marshal to North China to push them back. When it began looking as though the Young Marshal was not doing the job properly, the Generalissimo flew to North China and gave him a severe tongue lashing.

In a fit of temper, Chang Hsueh-liang permitted a group of Communist-influenced officers to dispatch a small force to the Generalissimo's quarters. They shot down his bodyguard. The Generalissimo jumped from his bedroom window to escape but hurt his back in the fall and was soon captured.

Madame Chiang Kai-shek, T. V. Soong, and Mr. Donald flew to North China and negotiated with the Young Marshal to release the Generalissimo, with the idea that they would all fly back to Nanking, where the Young Marshal would be given a prefunctory trial and released. The Central Government, however, did not consider this informal agreement binding. Back in Nanking, the Generalissimo resumed command, had the Young Marshal arrested and taken into protective custody as a political prisoner. Madame Chiang Kai-shek began nursing her husband back to health. To care for him and give treatments to his injured back, she called on her protégé, Caleb Chu, now a graduate nurse from Shanghai Sanitarium.

Elisabeth and Madame Chang Hsueh-liang did not know all these details at the time they were in London.

The strain of managing such a household, and the long weeks of caring for Raymond in the hospital began to take their toll on the health of the sturdy German nurse. The doctor said she must have a rest for her heart to quiet down and return to its normal function. She decided to go home for Christmas. In Ochsenhausen she found her father ill with a very weak heart. She wired her brother in America to come at once. On the fifth of January her father died.

Elisabeth cabled the Madame in England, explaining that she would not be able to return as soon as she had planned because of her father's death. No sooner was the funeral over than the Madame's daughter wired: "Please come at once. Mother wants to return to China."

"Wait for my letter," Elisabeth cabled. Then she wrote explaining that her brother was on his way to Germany, and that she must wait until he arrived because there were inheritance matters to be settled. It would be another week or two before she could come.

Back came another message from England. "We cannot do anything with mother. Please come at once." And so Elisabeth flew to England and tried to talk the Madame out of going immediately to China.

"If I don't go home now when my husband is in trouble, he will put me away and Miss Chow will be the number one wife," she wailed. "When he is in trouble, I must be there. I must go."

"I can't go with you to China," Elisabeth explained, "but I'll go as far as Genoa and see that you get on the ship."

In Genoa, the people from the embassy in Rome came to their aid, and Elisabeth put the Madame in the care of the ship's captain. She also made out all the tips for the stewards and stewardesses on the ship. Because the Madame could not read the menu, Elisabeth gave the table steward a list of "things the Madame will never eat," and a list of "things the Madame likes." She also sent word ahead for someone to meet the Madame in Singapore. When she had done everything she could to assure the Madame that she could make the journey safely, Elisabeth bade her good-bye and flew back to Germany.

And so ended Elisabeth's experience as traveling manager and nurse for the family of Chang Hsueh-liang.

Elisabeth diagnosed her weakness and chest pains as the result of an overworked heart. She went to the Tropical Institute at Tuebingen where her diagnosis was confirmed. "Complete rest for several weeks and then a light work load for several more months," the doctors prescribed.

Elisabeth wrote to the division office in Shanghai and to the General Conference in Washington telling them she could not return to China because she was unable to work.

She stayed on in Germany until 1938. During those months she thoroughly enjoyed the close association with her mother. But the beginning of political troubles in Germany and throughout Europe did not create a relaxing atmosphere for one who needed rest and recuperation. "I think it is time for me to go to America again," she told her mother. She soon sailed for New York, and on to Johnstown.

By the spring of 1939, she was feeling much better. She decided to go to Washington and take postgraduate work during the summer and return to work at the sanitarium in the fall.

While in Johnstown she gave a mission talk in church one Sabbath. The wife of one of the professors at the University of Pittsburgh heard her. She told her husband about it, and he asked Elisabeth if she would come to the Johnstown branch of Pittsburgh University and talk to the school. There a Presbyterian teacher asked her to talk at his church. Always happy to tell of the needs of China and to witness for the Lord, Elisabeth accepted the invitation. At the Presbyterian church some Methodist ladies asked her to talk at the mother-daughter dinner for their church. And so it went, from one church to another.

Elisabeth had not been in Washington very long before she received a letter from a Johnstown minister's wife inviting her to speak at a convention of Protestant ministers' wives being held in Washington. She talked to two different groups. Afterward women gathered around her plying her with questions, and asking, "Won't you come to my church to talk?" In no time Elisabeth was speaking to churches, women's clubs, and other groups, averaging three appointments a week. There is scarcely a church in the Washington area where she was not invited to speak—even for the Sunday morning church service in some places.

On three different occasions, to three different groups, she spoke in Peter Marshall's National Presbyterian Church. Catherine Marshall showed great interest in Elisabeth and offered to write Elisabeth's life story. Mrs. Marshall invited her home for tea on two or three different afternoons. With a secretary present, she interviewed the world-traveled nurse and made a rough draft for a book. Just at that time Madame Chiang Kai-shek came to Washington to ask the President and Congress for more aid for China. Elisabeth spent some time with the Madame. Then Elisabeth had to make a trip to Germany. All these interruptions interfered with the completion of the proposed book, and the project faded away.

Elisabeth spoke not only in churches, but also in Rotary Clubs, Lions Clubs, and university women's clubs. At that time people were keenly interested in China and in America's relations with that country. When asked her speaking "fee," Elisabeth always replied, "Enough to cover my transportation. Whatever else you care to give will be donated to the work in China." One Methodist church gave $100; some gave the evening's offering.

Elisabeth's health was fully restored. Besides her strenuous program of three lectures a week, she worked a regular eight-hour shift at the hospital. Normally, she didn't continue the lectures during the summer. But for three years, she spent the winter months lecturing. However, she was asked to speak one night in June, which turned out to be a very hot, muggy Washington night. One of her sister nurses seeing her hurrying around at the end of the work day asked, "Why are you rushing around so on a hot day like this?"

"I have a talk to give tonight."

"On a night like this! You've worked all day, and now going off to give a talk? Don't you have better sense?"

"I didn't know it was going to be so hot when I agreed to do it," Elisabeth said, fastening her dress while the perspiration ran down her back.

The Lutheran church where she was speaking that night was on the other side of the city. As she stood before the congregation, telling her story of China and its needs, she could feel the perspiration soaking through the back of her dress. There was no air conditioning in those days. But she told her story with the same enthusiasm as always. At the close of the meeting, the minister handed her two envelopes. "This is the evening's offering," he said.

When Elisabeth opened the envelopes she counted out $57. "You see," she told the nurse who had scolded her, "it was worth sweating for. I got $25 for Ingathering and the rest for China."

10

Back to the Orient

World War II dragged its sorrow-laden years across the world and ended with a mighty detonation. Hope sprang up in the hearts of missionaries, forcibly returned to their homelands or waiting in concentration camps. The General Conference began studying ways to get them back into the mission fields as soon as possible. Eager to go, Elisabeth awaited word that the State Department had cleared the way for women to return to China. Then came the Nürnberg interlude. At one time during her three and a half years in Germany the General Conference notified her that the way was now open for her to go to China. The General Conference suggested that she return to America and prepare to sail for Shanghai.

By now, however, Elisabeth had a new vision of her mission to Germany. "You can send someone else to China," she wrote in reply, "but I am perhaps the only one who can fill this particular niche in Germany at this time, keeping in touch with the German church and helping to funnel much-needed supplies to them." The General Conference agreed and sent someone else to China.

After her stint with the Army, Elisabeth returned to Washington.

SHANGHAI FALLS TO COMMUNISTS. With consternation she read the headlines on May 25, 1949. "Dear Lord," she prayed, "what will this mean to China and to Your work there?" One thing was certain, it meant that no missionaries could go to China now.

So once again Elisabeth settled down to a steady job of nursing at the Washington Sanitarium and Hospital. The weeks and months and years rolled by, and it looked as though Elisabeth Redelstein would end her working days where she had begun—at her alma mater.

Then Dr. Miller appeared with another surprise. "We're planning to start a hospital on Taiwan," he told her. "Would you be interested in helping us? You have the language and the experience, and you'd be of tremendous service."

"Of course, Dr. Miller, I'd be happy to go," she said. "But you know I'm sixty-three years old now, and they don't usually send out anyone at that age. Besides, I'm not sure I could pass the physical exam."

"Age doesn't matter!" The doctor's blue eyes twinkled. "I'm more than ten years older than you, and I'm not going to let that stop me!"

She passed the physical, the General Conference gave approval, and by early December she was on her way to Taiwan. She went by way of Europe so she could visit her family once more.

Arriving in Taipei, Taiwan, in February, 1955, she found problems awaiting her. She discovered that the people who had planned the wards were not medically oriented. The bedside tables were too small to hold a washbasin. There was no place to hang a towel near a bed. The mosquito netting, which had to be used at all times, was tied to bamboo sticks fastened to each bedpost.

Things were primitive in many ways, but the nursery was the worst of all. Elisabeth made drawings for the nursery units, but when the units came she found that her specifications had not been followed. Back to the carpenter shop she sent them for the necessary changes. She wondered how they would ever get the place ready for the official opening in March. Opening date was only a few weeks away. But everyone put in long hours, and they made it.

The day of the grand opening was clear and sunny. Baskets of flowers began arriving early in the morning with messages of congratulations from business houses and government offices. Arranged in the lobby and hallways, they filled the hospital with color and a delicate fragrance. Elisabeth checked on every detail. Chairs were arranged on the lawn for the guests, who began arriving at ten o'clock. The diplomatic corps and the premier of Taiwan occupied one section. A wide white ribbon with an immense bow stretched diagonally across the front door. Madame Chiang Kai-shek, Dr. Miller, the architect, and E. L. Longway (the mission director) sat on the flag-draped platform.

Each made a speech, and the Madame cut the ribbon with a pair of gold scissors. Dr. Miller led the way inside for a tour of the new facility. The guests couldn't help noticing that many things were needed to transform this new institution into a first-class hospital. Elisabeth heard them talking among themselves as they strolled along the halls. "Give Dr. Miller a little more time and a little more money, and he'll have this the best hospital on the island."

The new hospital opened for business. Miss Muriel Howe, an Australian nurse, trained at the Shanghai Sanitarium and with advanced studies in the United States, directed the training school. Elisabeth as head nurse had general charge of the hospital. Four graduate nurses from the Shanghai Sanitarium assisted her—one in charge of central supply, one general nurse, one night nurse, and one in charge of the pharmacy. Otherwise, she depended on student nurses and a few graduate nurses.

Among the first patients to apply for admission were several Americans who were serving in connection with the U.S. foreign aid program to Taiwan. These patients posed a new problem for Elisabeth. The hospital had only a Chinese cook, but these American patients wanted American food. There being nobody else to do it, Elisabeth took on the supervision of the foreign meals. She tried to meet every need whenever there was no one else to carry a particular load.

In the hospital from six o'clock in the morning until

eleven-thirty at night, Elisabeth kept a close watch on all procedures. Sometimes she would take a short siesta after lunch and return to the hospital about two-thirty in the afternoon.

Elisabeth considered eleven p.m. to be the most crucial time of the day, because it was so important to give full instructions to the night supervisor. Elisabeth always felt that the possibility of errors was great, since most of the help was unskilled. Surgery was usually scheduled for the morning, and Elisabeth wanted to make sure that the nurse understood the orders and that all preparatory procedures would be carried out. Not only did she tell the nurse, but she wrote out minute orders and pasted the medicines to the order sheet. "Of this you give so much," and "Of this you give so much." With all this precaution, no serious accidents ever happened. But there were some close calls.

One Chinese gentleman came in for a general check-up, and it was discovered that he had diabetes. The doctor ordered insulin for him, and Elisabeth put the insulin in the refrigerator. She sterilized a syringe and got it all ready. Then she said to the night nurse, "Here is the insulin, and here is the syringe. You give ten units of insulin in the morning. Do you understand?"

"Yes," the nurse replied. Elisabeth went home to an untroubled sleep. She awoke in the morning, however, with an insistent thought, "Call about that insulin shot." She got the nurse on the phone.

"You found that insulin syringe all right, didn't you, and you are going to give the shot?"

"I've already given it," the nurse replied, "but I couldn't use that syringe."

"What, you couldn't use that syringe!" Elisabeth said. "That syringe was in perfect order. There's no reason you couldn't use it."

"Yes, but I had to give ten units, and the syringe was too small."

"What do you mean?"

"Well, there were forty units in that ten CC and I had to give two and a half CC, and that syringe holds only one CC."

Elisabeth didn't waste any more words. She hung up and called another nurse whom she knew she could depend on. "The nurse who was looking after that diabetic patient gave him ten times the amount of insulin he should have had. Go at once and pour a big, tall glass of orange juice. Put in four medicine glasses of dextrose, stir it, and give it to the patient *immediately.*" Then she called the doctor.

"Give the man some orange juice and dextrose," he said.

As soon as she could get to the hospital, Elisabeth went to see the patient. "Sometimes when a patient has insulin for the first time," she told him, "he gets an unfavorable reaction. So if you start feeling sick, call me and we'll see what we can do." The man ate his breakfast, and afterward she gave him more orange juice and dextrose. The patient never knew he had been given ten times the amount of insulin he should have had. Elisabeth thanked the Lord for impressing her to call about the insulin and for the fact that the man did not go into insulin shock.

Supervising of the cooking of the American food was just too much for Elisabeth. When Mrs. Inez Longway returned from furlough, Elisabeth asked her to take over the job. Inez agreed to do it, and the two women worked closely together. Although they had known each other in Shanghai, a friendship now developed between them that Elisabeth declared to be the most enjoyable relationship she had ever known.

Not only did the American women in the city come as patients, they also came as volunteers. Every Monday afternoon several women came and made sponges and cotton balls. This was the first women's hospital volunteer corps Elisabeth knew of in the Orient. Their help was a real contribution to the hospital, and their friendship was greatly appreciated by Elisabeth and the rest of the hospital staff.

The Catholics had only a small, poorly equipped hospital on the island. So the priests and nuns came to the Taiwan Sanitarium whenever they needed physical attention. They were so impressed with the work they saw at the hospital that they offered to share some of the supplies they received from America.

The priest in charge of these supplies said, "You're training young people and you're doing a good work. We receive more supplies than we can use. Butterfat and powdered milk and things like that we'll gladly share with you." These items were hard to get, and Elisabeth appreciated the priest's generosity.

Madame Chiang Kai-shek shared things from America. Whenever she got celery or macademia nuts from Hawaii, she would send some over to Elisabeth. At Christmastime she sent six beautiful poinsettias. One of the poinsettias had nine blooms. Elisabeth often turned to the Madame for counsel.

One problem that the Madame eventually helped settle had to do with a young Chinese woman who came into the hospital for treatment. This young woman did not seem seriously ill. One evening as Elisabeth passed through the hall, she heard this patient say to her Chinese doctor, "Dr. Ling, why did I have to chew up that tablet? This morning you put one in my vagina, but this evening the nurse told me I had to chew it up."

"Oh, oh," Elisabeth thought, "I'd better see what goes on here."

"Wash out her stomach!" Dr. Ling ordered.

Elisabeth called the head doctor and told him what had happened. "That won't do her any harm at all," the doctor said. "It's only a mild, soothing tablet. It can't possibly do her any harm."

Elisabeth reported back to Dr. Ling, but he was determined to wash out the patient's stomach, and that got the patient all excited. The next day her boyfriend came to Elisabeth. "After what happened to my friend yesterday," he said, "I want you to put her in a private room."

And so into a private room she went, though it seemed to Elisabeth that there was nothing really wrong with her. A few hours later the boyfriend came again and said, "That room is so noisy, can't you put her in another room?" And so Elisabeth had her moved again.

The next day was Elisabeth's day off. When she returned to the hospital Thursday morning she was surprised to find the young woman in a semi-private room on the men's side of the hospital. "How did you happen to get in here?" Elisabeth asked. "I have a man patient coming in for this room this morning. We'll have to move you out. Who moved you in here anyway?"

"Oh, don't get excited, don't get excited," the young woman said. "My boyfriend moved me. We saw the empty room and so he just moved me in." Elisabeth promptly moved her out and called a maid to remake the bed with clean linen.

A few days later the newspaper carried a very critical article about the hospital. It said that the American nurse treated the patients like pieces of furniture, moving them three or four times within a few days–just like a piece of furniture. The article went on and on describing how this patient had been given medicine by the wrong method which resulted in having to pump her stomach and caused a great deal of suffering. The whole purpose of this newspaper story and other things the young man did was to get money from the hospital on the grounds of malpractice. One day in a confidential mood, the young woman told Elisabeth that she had been the most popular prostitute on the mainland.

Even though she and her boyfriend filed suit against the hospital, no one could get her to leave the place. Apparently she liked it there. She would leave in the morning but come back to spend the night. She went around telling the other patients how she had been given the wrong medicine or had it given in the wrong way. She caused the hospital no end of trouble. The hospital doctors agreed that nothing was wrong with her. Her boyfriend was in the army. His superior officers told him if he did not stop stirring up trouble he'd be dismissed from the army.

Finally, the hospital administrator told the young man, "All right, you have one of your army doctors come here and see the patient and get his opinion." The Madame, through the

Generalissimo, interceded with the army to do something to quiet this young couple. The army doctor came, a very fine Chinese gentleman. He was given the chart and all the records and told exactly what had happened. The patient was wheeled in in a wheelchair. She started right in telling the doctor loud and clear what the hospital had done to her. After a little while, the army doctor said, "That is enough, thank you," and she was wheeled from the room.

"Well, she seems to be in very good shape, if she can talk as loudly and wave her arms around as violently as that," the army doctor said. His report said the patient had recovered fully and needed no further hospitalization.

The hospital maintained a policy of accepting any patient they could possibly care for. One morning Elisabeth received a call from the U.S. Army Hospital. "The wife of one of our officers gave birth to a premature baby during the night. We can't take care of the infant here. Can you care for mother and child?"

"I'll ask the doctor and call you right back," Elisabeth promised.

"A premature baby would pose a real problem, because we have no incubator," she said to the doctor.

"Oh, I'm sure we can rig up something," he replied. "Let's not turn down any patients we can possibly help. Call the Army doctor back and tell him to send mother and child over right away. In the meantime you get a place ready for the infant in the nursery."

The young mother was friendly and easy to please. She never complained even though facilities were not the most up-to-date. The hospital had no laundry of its own. Laundry was sent to the school laundry. Elisabeth, however, thought baby laundry should be sterilized, and so the hospital set up a small laundry in one of the utility buildings and did the baby laundry there. Many times over the weekend the supply of clean diapers ran out, then Elisabeth went to the laundry and ironed the diapers in order to sterilize them. The father of the premature infant found out that she was doing this extra work.

"You shouldn't do that," he said. "The Army has a mangle they can let you have. One of the Americans left it with us when he went home. We don't use it, and if you'd like it we'll be glad to give it to you."

"Thank you so much," Elisabeth exclaimed. "That way I can sit down to iron the diapers and not have to be on my feet so much."

Twice a year Elisabeth ordered supplies from Hong Kong for use in preparing food for foreign patients. Army friends offered to buy anything that was needed at the PX. They kept her supplied with such items as flour, sugar, and Crisco. But other things had to be purchased in Hong Kong. One year Elisabeth spent her vacation in Hong Kong and decided to take advantage of the opportunity to buy supplies for the next six months. She also purchased some much-needed medical supplies. She was a little worried about the amount of duty she'd have to pay, but when she went through customs, the official asked, "This for the Longway Hospital?"

"Yes," Elisabeth answered.

"OK, OK." And she went on through with nothing more being said. E. L. Longway was widely known for his solicitation of funds to build the hospital. He made so many trips back and forth between Hong Kong and Taiwan, as superintendent of the South China Island Union Mission, that the customs officials all knew him.

Madame Chiang Kai-shek continued to be very friendly. One day after Elisabeth had been at the hospital for a year, the Madame called and said, "Isn't it time for you to go on vacation?"

"Yes, pretty soon."

"Where are you going?"

"I have no idea."

"How about coming up with us to our summer residence in the mountains?"

"That would be very nice, thank you."

"When can you come?"

"I don't know. I'll have to find out and let you know. I'll call you tomorrow."

Arrangements were made, and on the appointed date the Madame's chauffeur came for Elisabeth in the car and drove her to the Generalissimo's summer residence in the Yang Ming Shan (*Shan* in the word for mountain). Elisabeth was given one of the guest cottages, where she could relax. The Madame sent over her breakfast and then had her come to their house for dinner. In that beautiful quiet spot Elisabeth went for walks and enjoyed the birds and the trees. She read. She slept. And she visited with other vacationers. A Protestant Bible worker, Mrs. Twinem, occupied the cottage next to her. They found that they had much in common and enjoyed each other's company. One day Mrs. Twinem said, "Why don't we have our devotions together," and so every day they studied and prayed together.

The Madame belonged to a prayer group composed of prominent women on the island. Up on the mountain Sunday services were held for that group, and sometimes the Madame and Elisabeth would join them. On Sabbath Elisabeth attended the Adventist church, but on Sunday she enjoyed meeting with these other Christians.

The government brought professors from Purdue University to help the university in Taiwan. The leading professor's wife was a patient in the hospital for a time. Elisabeth looked after her diet, and the two of them became good friends.

"Any time you want to spend a quiet weekend," the professor's wife said, "don't hesitate to come to our place." Elisabeth accepted the invitation and got to know all of the professors and their families quite well.

Not only was the hospital successful in healing the bodies of the patients, but the nurses, practically all of whom were Seventh-day Adventists, were very good missionaries. The patients enjoyed the morning devotions. They heard the singing and remarked about it. At first morning worship was conducted in the chapel, but when the patients said they'd like to hear the whole service, the devotions were moved into the main lobby where they could all listen in. During Elisabeth's five years there, forty-five people were baptized as a result of their stay in the hospital.

One day the Madame called Elisabeth and said, "I've been feeling miserable and nervous. The doctor says that I need a good massage every now and then to relax me. Can you arrange for someone to give me a massage?"

"Madame, we really haven't anyone on our staff who can give a massage," Elisabeth explained. "You know how it is here. The Japanese when they were in control of the island trained all the blind men to be masseurs. So when we have a patient who needs a massage, we call one of the masseurs."

"Oh, that is out of the question. I wouldn't have a man give me a massage!"

"Although I haven't given massage in a long time, I'd be willing to give you one twice a week," Elisabeth said.

"Oh, as busy as you are that's out of the question."

"No, I'd consider it a privilege, and I'll be glad to do it."

And so it was arranged. Twice a week the chauffeur picked Elisabeth up at the hospital and drove her to the Madame's house.

In 1956 Dr. Miller decided to retire. He and his wife told close friends that they hoped to slip quietly away from Taiwan, but Elisabeth mentioned to the Madame that the doctor was leaving. "Oh, we'll have to do something special for him," the Madame declared. "I'll speak to my husband about it. I think he's entitled to the Blue Star of China, the highest decoration of the nation."

"Well, I'm not sure he'll accept it," Elisabeth cautioned. "You know the doctor's a very modest man."

"Don't worry. No one has ever refused it yet. Let's keep it a complete secret from the doctor!"

However, before the great day arrived, the doctor began to get inklings that something was stirring. When a courier came bringing a large red envelope containing the Generalissimo's invitation for luncheon "on March 26 at the President's mansion," Dr. Miller asked Elisabeth what she knew about it. She wouldn't say, but she could tell he was suspicious.

At the appointed time Dr. and Mrs. Miller, Dr. C. E. Randolph–the temporary replacement for Dr. Miller–and Elisabeth arrived at the mansion. They were ushered into an elegantly furnished room where a group of guests waited. When the Madame was announced, all the guests stood. Then the Generalissimo was announced, and again everyone stood. The Generalissimo chatted with the doctor, telling him how much he had learned to like soy milk since the doctor had prescribed it for his stomach trouble years before. After the luncheon, the Madame led the way into the living room. There the Generalissimo made a little speech, telling the doctor how much his years of service to China had been appreciated. He ended by saying that the government had authorized him to present its highest decoration. Opening a little red case, he took out a gold medal and pinned it on the doctor's coat. He then took a scroll and solemnly unrolled it. It was inscribed by the president, the foreign minister, and the minister of defense. The Generalissimo read it in Chinese and then asked his secretary to read a translation in English for the benefit of the foreign guests. Photographers were everywhere, and flashbulbs popped as they took pictures of Dr. Miller and the group.

Although Dr. Miller had "retired," he did not stop working. Before long he was going from one needy mission hospital to another throughout the world field, filling in whenever a doctor became ill or had to go on furlough. Occasionally his trips brought him back to the Orient. One December morning in 1958 he flew in from Japan to spend a few days on Taiwan. Mr. and Mrs. W. L. Hilliard, treasurer of the South China Island Union Mission, took Elisabeth with them to the airport to meet the doctor. Mrs. Hilliard invited them to her house for breakfast.

While they were eating, a telegram arrived addressed for Elisabeth. She read: "This Is Your Life program. We are featuring Dr. Caleb Chu on our program, and we hear that you have had quite an influence on his life. We'd like you to be on the program with him. We've already contacted the General Conference, and they approve our going ahead. We've contacted the authorities there, and they say you should go to the American Embassy and contact them. We're also arranging transportation for your flight. All we need is your OK."

Bewildered, Elisabeth handed the telegram over to Dr. Miller. "What shall I do?" she asked.

"Of course you'll go!"

"Dr. Miller, I've only been back from vacation in Japan about two months, and now to leave again?"

"This is a once-in-a-lifetime thing. I'll explain it to the folk at the sanitarium. You'd better go right down and send a telegram that you'll accept the invitation."

Within a few days Elisabeth was on her way across the blue Pacific to America and the This Is Your Life program. Elisabeth had never flown first-class before. When she looked at her ticket and saw the cost, $1400, she thought, "What an awful lot of money! What a lot of good it could do for the mission!"

Arriving in Hollywood, she was met by a woman from the program who took her to the hotel where all the guests were staying. On the way to the hotel the woman said, "I understand that most of the Adventists are vegetarians. Can you give me some suggestions that I can pass on to the cook at the hotel for vegetarian dishes?" This was not hard for Elisabeth to do.

At the hotel she met old friends from China who also had played a part in Caleb Chu's life. Josephine Cunnington Edwards had suggested Dr. Chu's name to Ralph Edwards after she had learned about the doctor's work among the poor people in the hills of Kentucky. And here they all were waiting for the program and talking about how surprised Caleb would be. Elisabeth learned of the ruse that had been used to lure Caleb to California. He'd been invited to come to the College of Medical Evangelists at Loma Linda (now Loma Linda University) to talk to the senior medical students about locating in the needy areas of the United States.

The day the program was to be filmed, his good friend, Abraham Liu, also a graduate of Shanghai Sanitarium and now a doctor on the staff at Loma Linda, said to Caleb, "There's a special program on in Hollywood this afternoon. Dr. Godfrey Anderson, the college president, and I are going, and we'd like you to come along."

Of course Dr. Chu accepted the invitation. The three doctors sat in the audience, while the participating guests for the program watched the proceedings on a monitoring screen behind a curtain.

Ralph Edwards walked out into the audience and began talking, "Tonight we have the story of a very interesting life," he said. "In fact, it could almost be called two lives, for the young man who is our guest was once a member of Chiang Kai-shek's household. Then he took the nurses' course and finally became a doctor." Watching behind the curtain, Elisabeth saw Caleb begin to fidget and look questioningly at Abraham Liu. Just then Ralph Edwards strolled up to him and said, "Tonight, Dr. Caleb Chu, This Is Your Life."

Caleb Chu had never heard of the This Is Your Life program, and in a daze he permitted himself to be led to the platform. The drama rose to an emotional peak when his brother from Hong Kong, whom he had not seen for nine years, walked out onto the stage. Caleb regained his composure in a moment and happily greeted all his other friends as one by one they came to the stage, each telling some incident in the doctor's life.

Elisabeth already knew how Caleb had become a doctor, for Madame Chiang Kai-shek had told her. After he had nursed the Generalissimo and helped him to recover from his back injury, the Madame asked him if he wouldn't like to take the medical course. "Oh, that would be wonderful," Caleb said, "but I have not had premed."

"I think you can get into the Nanking Medical School by passing the entrance exam whether you have had premed or not." So Caleb set about studying premed subjects, but he failed the examination. However, the Madame persuaded the school officials to give him a try anyway. "If he can't make his grades by the end of the first year," she said, "I won't ask you to carry him any longer."

By the end of that first year his grades assured his acceptance for the second year. At the end of four years he received his M.D. degree.

He then became a doctor at the Lanchow Hospital in far Northwest China. The Madame asked him if he'd like to go to America to study further. She said she would arrange it, but he said, "I couldn't let the mission down. I'm needed at Lanchow."

In spite of the fighting, Caleb stayed.

The time came when it seemed imperative to leave, but for a long time he resisted the urge to flee. "I can't leave the patients," he said again and again. When it looked as though the last opportunity had passed, the people of Lanchow were surprised to see one lone plane swoop down at their airport. Some mission body had shipped a planeload of Bibles into Lanchow. The pilot said he'd be glad to take passengers on his return trip. Caleb Chu and his family were quickly put aboard and flown to Hong Kong. From there he went to America. He worked in surgery at Philadelphia's Jefferson Memorial Hospital, which earned him membership in the American College of Surgeons.

The This Is Your Life program highlighted some of these facts. His private practice in rural Kentucky made a name for him, not only as a good doctor, but also as a man who loved people. He helped in every way he could the people of that mountain area.

No one was prouder of Caleb than Elisabeth. She only wished that the Madame could have been there to share this moment with him. This Is Your Life paid Elisabeth's fare to Berkeley to visit friends over New Year's Day. On the third of January, after a three-week absence, she flew back to Taiwan.

When it came time for Elisabeth to return to America in 1959 after nearly five years in Taiwan, she began receiving letters from former students all over the Orient. The letters came from the Philippines, Hong Kong, and even Burma. The general tenor of them all was, "Miss Redelstein, you probably won't come back to the Orient again, so on your way home please try to stop off here."

In the Philippines she found a dozen or more of her former students. In Hong Kong there were graduates of both Shanghai and Taiwan. In Singapore her friends got together for a real celebration. She talked to the students at the school and reported on the progress of the work in Taiwan.

Spending a weekend in Burma was an exciting experience, for she had never been there before, and it was not easy for foreigners to gain admittance to that land. At Beirut, Lebanon, she was the guest of Elder and Mrs. Raymond Hartwell, with whom she had been in language school in Shanghai away back in 1927. Elisabeth experienced that greatest reward of any teacher as she saw what her former students and associates were doing. Perhaps her reward was even more precious than that of the average teacher, for she found her students preaching Christ to the world.

After another visit with her family in Europe, it was back to America, where she worked again at the Washington Adventist Hospital. Asked what department she preferred to work in, Elisabeth chose maternity, and she volunteered to work the three to eleven shift. "I know you have a hard time getting nurses to work that shift," she told the supervisor, "because the young girls want their evenings free to be with their boyfriends, and I think the young mothers should be home with their families in the evening." For five years she worked this shift in the one hospital department that throbs with life and happiness.

Dr. Chu's wife was killed in an automobile accident. After Elisabeth went to the funeral and saw the situation he was in with three children and no one to help him, she resigned from the hospital and went to keep house for the doctor and care for the children. His children called her "Grandma." After several months, when she was sure his situation was well in hand, she returned to Takoma Park. Now in her early 80's she still lives there, keenly interested in all that goes on and eager to do everything she can to lend a helping hand. She can still hold an audience of friends spellbound with the recital of experiences through which the Lord led her as China Nurse.

Family picture taken in September, 1911, just before Elisabeth left for America. Standing, left to right: Father, Walter, Elisabeth, Hubert, Max. Seated: Albrecht and Mother. Hubert and Albrecht were killed in World War I.

The foreign students of one of the early graduating classes of Shanghai Sanitarium, two Koreans and the rest from the Philippines. Doctor Harry Miller, center back; Elisabeth Redelstein, center front.

Madame Chiang Kai-shek.

The family of Chang Hsueh-liang. From left: Pauline, Raymond, Martin, Madame Chang. Photo taken while the family was in England.

Madame Chang Hsueh-liang and Elisabeth.

Elisabeth and Madame Chiang Kai-shek on the opening day of the Taiwan Sanitarium.

Happy mother and father despite the cries of their new-born infant. The doctors had feared they would lose either the mother or the baby. A proud nurse Elisabeth holds the baby.

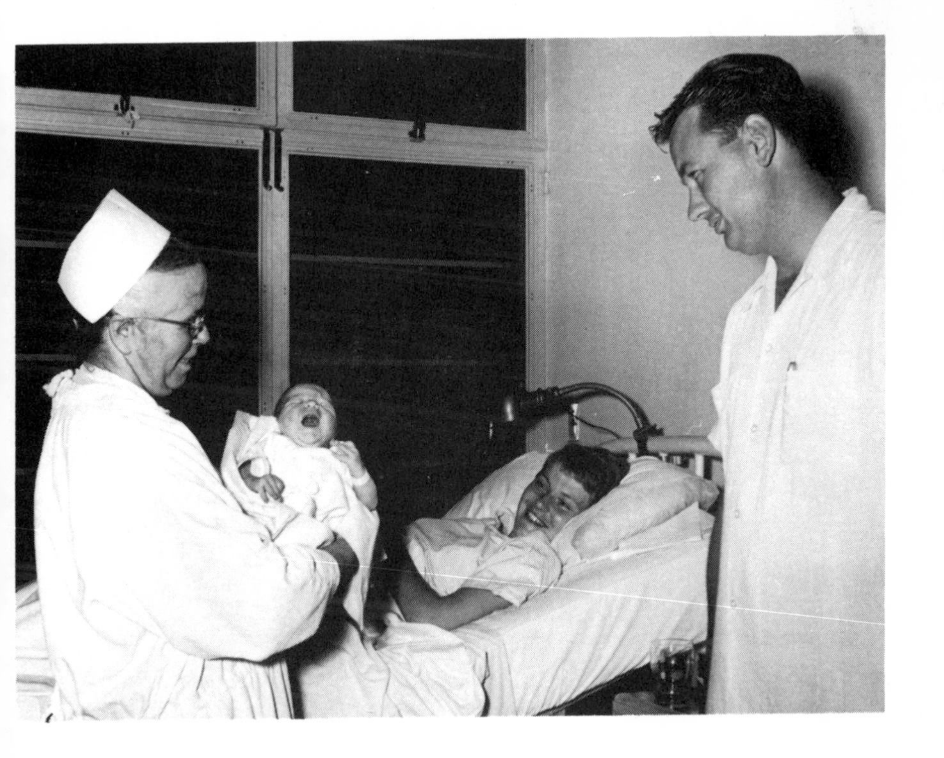

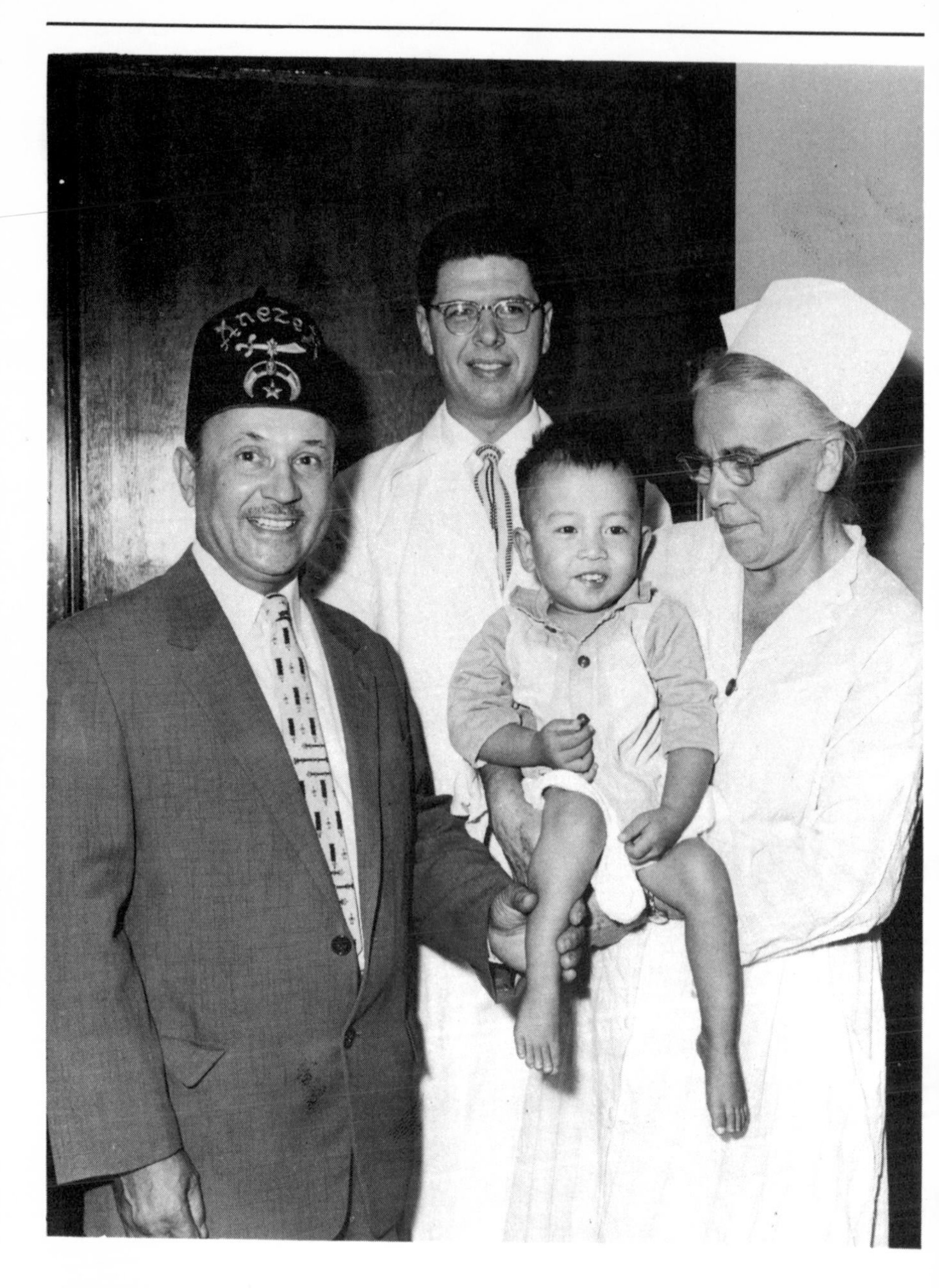

The Shriners supported one bed in the Taiwan Sanitarium for polio cases. Here a proud Shriner, Doctor Mitchell, and nurse Elisabeth display a happy polio victim. Notice that Miss Redelstein never wore stripes on her cap. She considered stripes a mark of rank.

Left to right: President Chiang Kai-shek, Dr. C. E. Randolph, the secretary reading the citation, Elisabeth, the Madame, Doctor Miller, Mrs. Miller, at the time the highest decoration of the Nationalist Chinese government was conferred on Doctor Miller in 1956.

雷女士

蔣中正

Personally autographed photograph of Chiang Kai-shek.